# Life of a Common Man
## With a Praying Mom

*Sterling Sparks*

Printed in the United States of America by **Sterling Sparks.**

First Printing
**paperback ISBN:** 978-1-7339240-7-8
**hardback ISBN:** 978-1-7339240-9-2
**ebook ISBN:** 978-1-7339240-8-5

Cover:   JD&J Design, LLC
Interior:  Gary L. Jenkins

Dedicated life to Lilyrene Sparks, someone who prayed for me
throughout my life.


Thanks to her prayers, I'm still here.

# Table of Contents

*"Honor thy father and mother, the first commandment with promise that it may go well with thee and you may live long upon the earth." (Eph 6:2-3, KJV)*

# Foreword

Since a doctor told my expectant mother that the baby she carried would not live, my journey has been one of faith. At first, my parent's faith sustained me. From my earliest recollection, they prayed aloud for me and encouraged me to know the Lord they held so dear. While times of trouble and blessing came and went, I found their advice to be a valuable gift.

Growing up with few resources in rural Kentucky, I learned the importance of hard work and perseverance from the youngest age. Family was everything back then, it continues to mean the world to me. The Sparks clan stuck together through moves, marriages, and many moods. Love is bond that isn't easily broken. Quit is not a word that my parents allowed into our vocabulary. If any of us children started a task, our obligation was to see it through to the end.

Goals are easy to set, but not always easy to achieve. Like everyone, my life includes battles where the outcome seemed majorly in doubt. Yet, faith in God keep me on the right track and eventually I accomplished whatever goal lay before me.

This book is about encouragement. If you are going through a difficult challenge, I can relate. In my decades long military career, I had to compete for jobs, train for harsh conditions, and work like crazy to earn promotions.

Part of my success only came because I refused to take no for an answer. By sticking to my guns, I feel like I've gotten the most out of life. My new goal is help you do the same.

Come along for the ride as I find my way from a remote county in Kentucky to much more opportunity in Ohio. Walk with me through the awkward moments of teachers determined to help me "talk right." Share my teenage triumphs of learning to sell magazine subscriptions and mastering the cash register (as a left-handed person) when required to use my right hand.

Without giving away the best parts of my story, suffice it to say that life got tough many times. I didn't do everything right, and even suffered through a time when my faith seemed inadequate for life's difficulties.

In times good and bad, my sweet mom prayed for me. Even after my parents and two of my siblings moved to Ohio, we never stopped going back to Kentucky to reunite with family and friends. In an incredible gift, my sister bought my parent's former farmhouse providing a familiar backdrop for family reunions and homecomings. This bond of family is worth fighting for even through the dark seasons of life.

May your heart be filled with the love that marks each stage of a life well lived. Whether an optimist like myself or someone who sees the risk before the opportunity, may you be blessed with the persistence to achieve all of your godly dreams.

# 1

What I'm about to tell you might sound strange, but I can assure you it's all true. Hang in there, and you just might believe that miracles are not only possible, but happen every day.

The old pick-up rattled and jerked along the rough road to Ravenna, Kentucky. Lilyrene Sparks clutched her stomach and tried not convulse into the dry heaves again. Rain drizzled onto the windshield, and James tried to concentrate on the road ahead. What I'm about to tell you might sound strange, but I can assure you it's all true.

On another day, the orange, yellow, and red leaves might have commanded his attention. With a very sick wife in the truck next to him and deer as likely as not to come bolting out of the woods, James prayed and stared intently at the road ahead of him.

Lilyrene felt relief that help was on the way. She didn't know the origin of this mysterious illness, but her insides felt like they might come out at any moment. Surely, the only doctor within thirty miles would offer sage advice and something to relieve her pain.

Mind you, James and Lilyrene didn't spring for a doctor bill lightly. Like most of their neighbors, cash money didn't float their way often in 1946 America. They'd heard of a coming post-war boom, but nothing was booming yet in their neck of the woods. Everyone struggled to put food on the table, pay their rent or mortgage, and put clothes on their backs. Hard work filled up most of their days. With no running water or central heat, the simplest tasks took hours to complete.

Finally, the first few houses of town showed up ahead of them. Though the houses appeared modest by most standards, Ravenna had its charms. Large deciduous trees and a backdrop of mountains gave the village a storybook aura that Lilyrene adored. They made this trip at least once a week for church and more often if James' job at the railroad allowed.

The borrowed truck slid into the small gravel lot in front of Doc Marcum's white wood-frame house. Walking around to side of the home, James supported his wife with an arm around the small of her back. Just above the side door, a small sign read simply "Office." He barely had time to knock before the kind country doctor opened the door. Doc Marcum must have heard the truck on the gravel, Lilyrene supposed.

"Come in, come in."

"Thank you, Doc," James said. "My wife is feeling poorly,

been ejecting her insides all night and this morning some too."

"Okay, you stay out in the lobby, and I will take a look at her in the examining room."

Doc Marcum's office consisted of just two rooms. The first was an unheated sunroom with three kitchen chairs sitting along the wall. An adjoining room held an examining table, a stool on wheels, and a white, metal cabinet about four feet tall. A few glass containers sat atop the cabinet and held things like cotton balls and tongue depressors. A simple black frame on the wall held Doc Marcum's medical school diploma.

Lilyrene dreaded having the doctor examine her. She'd given birth five times, each at home with the help of a midwife. One of her children died at a year old, so only four were still living. That must have been as God intended, although she would never know why.

The Sparks family had no money for fancy hospitals, but neither did most of the county's population. The area barely supported their own doctor, and most people felt thankful to have him. Now, a man she knew by reputation and by only a few brief encounters in town would be examining her. Quite embarrassing.

"Alright, Mrs. Sparks. Take off your coat and hang it on the hook behind the door. I'm going to listen to your heart."

The stethoscope felt cold against her cotton dress. The doctor listened in several different places on her chest and her back. She found it highly irregular that he would listen to her back to hear her heartbeat. She wondered if he could be trusted.

Doc Marcum took her temperature. What came next embarrassed her beyond measure. Let's just say, after many questions and the examination, he invited Lilyrene to get into her clothes, shoes, and coat while he talked to her husband.

The loose-fitting door to the outer office did little to muffle the sound of the conversation between James and the doctor, particularly after the first two or three sentences.

"You want us to do what?" James exclaimed loudly.

"Look, your wife is pregnant again. She is not well. Based on her physical condition and her medical history, I assure you she cannot carry a healthy child to term. Either she or the baby will suffer calamitous effects. My recommendation is that you take Lilyrene immediately to Patty A. Clay Hospital in Richmond. They can induce labor before this pregnancy advances any further."

"No way, doc," James said. "We are not going to have no abortion!"

"Now James, I'm offering you sound medical advice. If Lilyrene tries to continue with this pregnancy, she may well be dead within a few months. Who is going to look after you and the rest of the kids if that happens?"

"What exactly are you saying?" James shouted.

Lilyrene could hear the anger building in James' voice. Knowing her husband so well, it wouldn't be long until the relatively civil conversation got louder, and things might be said that neither man could take back. Lilyrene skipped fastening the last couple of buttons on her coat and grabbed her purse.

"Honey, is everything alright?" she asked as she opened the door from the examining room. As she had envisioned, the color on James' face burned red, and his nostrils flared.

"Mrs. Sparks, I was just telling your husband that I advise against you continuing with this pregnancy. Your health and that of the fetus is not good. If you try to carry it to term, there is a very good chance you and/or the baby will surely die."

Lilyrene just looked at James. She knew what his answer would be, and she felt the same way. His face morphed from anger to stone-cold determination. Like flint, his features got that look which meant a stubborn man would not be changing his mind.

"Look, Doctor Marcum, my wife and I just don't believe in abortion. God sends the babies, and we are going to trust Him with Lilyrene's life and the life of our unborn child. That's the end of the story. Now how much do I owe you?"

"I wish you would listen to me and at least take her to the hospital for more formal testing." Doc Marcum's faced pleaded, but resignation began to creep across his features. He sighed, looked down, and took a step back from the couple.

"How much?" James said, looking resolute and stern with a jaw set like stone.

"That will be two dollars."

Lilyrene opened her purse and slowly took out a bag with a drawstring. The contents of her small handbag totaled exactly $2.00. She whispered a small prayer under her breath and extracted two one-dollar bills.

On the ride back to the house, she felt somewhat better. There was no good reason for her to feel any improvement, but perhaps just avowing their trust in God's healing power worked the miracle. She thought about Doctor Marcum and wondered about his eternal soul. Such a good man in the way he treated people, but his medical training may have overridden his conscience. Although his advice in this case didn't line up with Lilyrene's view of the Bible, she certainly didn't judge Doc Marcum's soul.

His good-hearted ways reflected a man committed to taking care of Kentucky people with little means.

He often took much less money than should have been due him. After one of the Sparks children suffered a lengthy illness and required weeks of medicine and treatment, the bill should have totaled $400 or more. No one in the county had that kind of money. When James went into the office to discuss payment terms, Doc Marcum said there must have been a mistake. The bill totaled only twenty dollars. "The rest of the bill must have got lost" is what he told James.

Abortion is not an option for those who follow Christ. Lilyrene felt sure about that fact. James prayed aloud as they bounced along the country roads. "Lord, we are just going to trust you for this baby. Whether he or she is born alive or not, we know you want Lilyrene to do her best to bring this little life into the world. Heal my wife. Nourish this baby. Do your miracles. We trust in You!"

Exactly thirty-two weeks later in Camel's Branch, Kentucky, Lilyrene gave birth to an 11-pound, 12-ounce monster of a baby. They named him Sterling. That's me! Not only did the doctor's advice prove incorrect, but I've survived quite well these past seventy-three years. Thank you, Daddy and Mom for believing in God more than in doctors. Your prayers and faith gave me life.

If I sound proud of Daddy and Mom, that's an understatement. Dad worked very hard to take care of his family. When I was born, he regularly walked six miles to work at the railroad. He might do a sixteen-hour shift, then walk back home. My siblings tell me that first house was quite modest. Without a refrigerator, they kept our milk in the creek to keep it cold.

My older sister, Cathalene, had the honor of taking

my poopy diapers to the creek, washing them along with other pieces of our family's meager wardrobe. Hopefully, she washed downstream from the "refrigerator." She still reminds me of her diaper duty every so often. It must have made quite an impression on her. In those days, almost no one we knew had an electric washing machine. It wouldn't have mattered if we did, as the family enjoyed no indoor plumbing.

My father's diligent attempts to support our family shaped my childhood in many ways. About two years after I was born, he moved the family to Richmond, Kentucky, about thirty-five miles away from Ravenna. He and my brothers, who were just entering puberty, worked long hours growing and harvesting tobacco. In those days, landowners would allow men like my father to farm part of their acreage in exchange for a share of the crop, thus the term sharecropper. Daddy heard from some friends that several farmers near Richmond had more land than they could farm. By renting out some of the land, both the farmers and the sharecroppers, theoretically at least, could make some money. Dad and my older brothers Woody and Ray planted tobacco, which has always been a staple of the Kentucky economy.

Woody and Ray helped plant, weed, and harvest the tobacco. Though hard work, the rewards at harvest time seemed to offset the pain of working in the fields through the hot summers.

In 1950, when I was three years old, I got sick. Relatives tell me that I spiked a high fever and eventually lapsed into a coma. Although my parents tried to avoid major medical expenses, this illness required drastic action. Daddy took me to Patty A. Clay Hospital. They ran some tests and didn't offer much hope for recovery. A grim-faced doctor stood over my bed. "We are sorry, Mr. and Mrs. Sparks, there is nothing else we can do. Sterling may not recover," the doctor intoned.

Having already lost a one child, my mother realized life sometimes dealt harsh blows. Not panicked, but deeply concerned, she found a quiet place to pray. Down on her knees at the hospital, she prayed, "Lord, you gave us little Sterling, and we will sure miss Him. We give his life back to You, if that's what is required. It's Your decision if he lives or dies. We don't trust in doctors. We believe in You. Say one word, and it will be done. Let our little boy be healed by Your amazing power, and I will give You the glory."

Rising from her impromptu altar, Mom later told me that she felt calm. Whatever the outcome, peace flooded into her soul. She made her way back to my hospital room. When she'd left just minutes before, I was in a deep coma. When she returned, I was sitting up and smiling.

"Mom," I said. "I'm starved. Can I get something to eat?"

"Yes, honey," she said. "I imagine you can."

My parents prayed and lived by their faith. Throughout my childhood, prayer remained a regular fixture at church and in our home. Many nights, sitting around the house, we would sing gospel songs or just listen while Mom or Daddy talked about the Lord. Their faith kept us all on the right track back then.

After a couple of years, Daddy decided that sharecropping was not for him. He and my brothers worked hard, but the rewards were not worth the effort. When they received their share of the tobacco crop that second year in Richmond, they sold the tobacco and moved back home. Daddy heard of a place for sale near in Cow Creek, Kentucky, near where we lived before. He found a house in the country with a little land, planning to farm and raise a few animals. The house had more room than our previous two-room place, and the soil seemed better suited to growing vegetables.

When asked if we had running water at that house, I answer, "Yes, my brother and I run out back, pulled the water up out of the well, and run back in the house with it. That was our running water."

In 1952, I became quite ill again. This time, God intervened before my parents sought medical attention for me. Uncle Bert lived just a few miles down the road. One day, he felt a strong urge to walk over to our house, but he wasn't sure why. As a believer, he listened when the Holy Spirit prompted him. In short order, he showed up unannounced on our front porch. (We didn't have a phone yet.)

"Hello, Burt, what brings you over this way?" Mom asked.

"Lilyrene, good to see you. Well, I was out in the woods working. All morning, I kept having this feeling like the Holy Ghost telling me I needed to come over here. Could anyone use some prayers?"

"Well, yes. Little Sterling is sick with a fever and not feeling well at all. Come on in the house," my mom said. "He's in the bed."

I heard my uncle's footsteps, but I didn't know who it was until he poked his head into the room. Dressed like always in a flannel shirt and non-descript blue pants, he smiled at me.

"How are you doing, Sterling?" Uncle Burt asked.

"I feel sick. My stomach hurts. I'm kind of cold even with these blankets."

Uncle Burt sat on the side of my twin bed. He reached down and felt my forehead. "You are burning up with fever. When we have a high fever, it can make the rest of our body feel cold. Sterling, I feel like God told me to come over here and pray with you. You know God loves you and cares about you, right?"

"Yeah," I said. "I know."

"We are going to pray, and I believe Jesus will heal you," Uncle Burt said in his normal speaking voice. Soon he would be praying in his loud praying voice. "Dear Lord, we pray right now for Sterling. Come right here in this room and take away his sickness. We believe by the stripes you took for us on your back, this little boy is going to get up from this bed completely well. Heal him in the name of Jesus!" Toward the end of his prayer, Uncle Burt clapped his hands loudly.

When he finished praying for me, I knew God had healed me in a supernatural way. Soon after he finished praying, I felt much better. Within the hour, I sat fully clothed and ate a late breakfast.

To understand our family, you need to realize that faith infused everything we did back then. We spent considerable time at a church where everyone prayed out loud at the same time. As the Spirit moved, it got a little rowdy sometimes. I suppose you could call us holy rollers, though no one rolled around on the floor that I can remember. Simple country folks, we had the audacity to just believe the Bible as God's Word. All of us trusted strongly in the power and ability of our Savior to heal, to change lives, and to protect us from the many perils that befall the poor. This gave us courage to live in a fragile world.

Dad's vision for our house at Cow Creek centered on growing vegetables and tending chickens and hogs. We raised the hogs and sold six or seven sows per year, keeping a couple for our own use. When the hogs reached market weight, Dad would borrow someone's trailer for hauling livestock. He took a half dozen hogs at a time to the market in Richmond, selling them at auction.

Raising hogs paid some of the bills and gave us money for other staples. I would have loved to go with Daddy to the hog market, but he didn't want children slowing him down when on a mission. Who knows? We might have asked to stop on the way and pee or something. Always mission focused, he lived by the credo that the closest way from here to there is a straight line.

In retrospect, I'm not sure his style represented the best model for parenting, but Daddy had a lot to think about and much to get done. He worked hard from sunup to sundown. It's easy for me to understand his laser focus on providing for all of us kids and Mom.

Each spring, Daddy would climb down into our well, basically a hole in the ground, not far behind the house. He would dig out all the dirt and crawdads. Mud would gather and eventually make it hard to collect enough water for our family. We didn't have a pump. Instead, we just let a bucket down and collected water from the bottom of the well.

Daddy augmented our natural filtration system (soil) with Clorox. After cleaning out the well, he would emerge looking a little worse for wear. Then, he would dump a significant amount of Clorox down the well and let it sit for several hours. Later that day, we could start drinking the water again.

As young as six years old, I began making water runs out back. Once the bucket was filled about three-fourths of the way to the top, I'd carefully bring it back in the house. Soon, I graduated to two buckets, one in each hand. Mom pressed my brother Phil into service just a year after me.

I remember one of my sisters saying, "Those are big buckets for small boys." We didn't mind as the chore soon became a regular part of life. It felt good to contribute something to the family.

Our running water duty happened twelve months a year in every kind of weather. My siblings and I took in stride all the work around the house without a lot of complaining. After all, the country lifestyle became all we knew at that point. Although Kentucky is not Alaska, we had many days below freezing each year. Fortunately, the water in the well (several feet below ground) didn't freeze. In the house, the water bucket sat on a counter in the kitchen. Everyone in the family (and any visitors) used the same dipper to scoop out a drink, consume it, and put the dipper back in the bucket. I guess that era represented a time before germs or proper hydration were fully understood.

Back then, children did tasks that would astound and perhaps horrify adults today. As a six-year-old, I would get up early and make my way to the kitchen. My jobs included putting a piece of coal or a couple of pieces of wood in the metal stove. Then, I'd dip a piece of paper in kerosene (which we called coal oil.) These days, we can't imagine a six-year-old getting up alone and being in charge of starting a fire. But after lighting the paper, I threw it into the stove and closed the metal door. None of us burnt the house down or disfigured ourselves, so I guess responsibility can be learned at a young age.

Daddy tried many things to earn money and raise our family's standard of living. We never went without the basics, but none of us had many possessions. In his search for the pot of gold in life, Daddy never shied away from trying new things. He attempted every available means to keep us fed and clothed. From time to time, he would hitchhike the four-hour car trip to Ohio to try to get a construction job. In that post-war era, the government put a lot of people to work building the nation's highway system. In the Dayton and Cincinnati areas, roads, houses, and other buildings sprouted up likes weeds after a spring rain. Although a lengthy car ride, Daddy could get rides up there relatively easily. In a week or two, he would send money back to Mom and us kids. We hated being away from him but understood the necessary sacrifice. Each time, he returned as a conquering hero to us. His pockets bulged with small treats of fruit or candy. When Daddy came home, everything seemed right with the world again.

*"The Lord is my rock, and my fortress, and my deliverer; my God, my strength, in whom I will trust; my buckler, and the horn of my salvation, and my high tower"*
*(Psalm 18:2).*

# 2

One of the best things about growing up in a large family is the companionship. No matter how difficult or tiring the task, it seemed easier when working with a buddy. My two older brothers, Ray and Woody, partnered up for chores that required more brawn than my six-year-old self could handle. My younger brother, Jerry Phillip—we called him Phil—became my closest companion. We had many adventures in the rural area where we lived.

One summer day, Phil and I went exploring in the woods. We came upon a yellow jacket nest in the ground. Most people think all stinging bees and wasps make their nests or hives up high. However, I can tell you from experience that yellow jackets often nest in the ground, preferring the cool temperatures in the hot Kentucky summers. Once Phil and I got a good look at the nest, we decided discretion would be the better part of valor. Several yellow jacket sentries buzzed in our direction sending us fleeing the scene. As I ran, my foot caught on something, and I lost my balance and toppled to the ground. Phil looked back to see what happened. Down I went on a jagged piece of tin as I fell. My knee burst open and quickly shrouded my lower leg in blood. Phil collected me and we made our way back to the house. One of my sisters shrieked as I entered bleeding.

Today, such a wound would have indicated an emergency room visit and at least fifteen stitches. Mom calmly cleaned the cut with water and a rag. She packed the entire length of the incision with salt to prevent infection and stop the escaping blood. Her homespun medical treatment worked. She bandaged my leg and sent me on my way, not the first or last time. Mom's loving way of doctoring kept us all going most of the time. In this case, my leg healed fine and didn't become infected, but it left me a lengthy scar to show off to anyone interested enough to look.

Although Christmas wasn't as big a deal as it became later in our lives, the memories remain special ones. We didn't have much in the way of material goods, but love overflowed from that farmhouse. At some point in December, Daddy would take us out in the woods and cut down a cedar tree. Mom would make popcorn on the stove. We used needle and thread to sew strings of garland to adorn our Christmas tree. Someone always made a star out of tinfoil and cardboard, or whatever we had handy. We dressed the tree with little bits of crepe paper Mom saved throughout the year. Before long, our living room looked a lot like Christmas.

Inevitably, Daddy would find work in Ohio during the days leading up to the December holiday. When he got back from his trip, he brought Christmas gifts, including the one we enjoyed the most: a big fruit basket. Nowadays, fruit is more common and not appreciated in the same way. Back then, fruit in the winter felt like luxury.

Each child might get a banana, an apple, an orange, and maybe a handful of grapes. Remember that fruit did not grace our table most of the year. Daddy brought another most treasured gift. We each received our own pack of chewing gum. Five whole pieces of gum to be enjoyed whenever we decided to chew it. With no mini market nearby, our own candy or gum served as a big treat. In the good years, each child also got our favorite candy bar if Daddy could find it. The one I loved the most, Three Musketeers, sent me into ecstasy from the first bite to the last. I made it last a long time.

Daddy also tried to bring home mixed nuts and a five-pound box of peppermint candy. As we sat around the fire at night, he would chop up the peppermint candy a little at a time. Each child got a piece to suck on while Mom read a short Bible story or Daddy told us about an adventure in Ohio. We sang Christmas songs or hymns. These times felt like pure gold, just being together with everyone.

One of the best features of that home included a great chicken house that my father and brothers built out back. The chicken hotel had two rooms. The laying hens hung out on one side and the rooster stayed on the other side most nights. Each year, my daddy ordered a hundred chicks from Farmer's Home Supply. The four boys took turns caring for the chicks.

In the hen house, the chickens drank from a gallon

water jug turned upside down and outfitted with a feeder tip on the bottom. Whenever a chicken got thirsty, they could just walk over and get a drink. The water needed to be refilled twice a day and cleaned out regularly to keep the chickens healthy. Similarly, there was a feed jug. The feed store sold cracked corn in eighty- or one-hundred-pound bags. Our role included dipping out a portion of chicken feed and filling up the feeder jug. Lots of fresh water and plenty of feed kept our chicks healthy and growing fast.

Not long after we got the chickens one March, the weather turned unusually cold. Chicks must be kept warm or they die. So, Woody and Ray slept in the chicken house to make sure the stove kept them warm all night. Chicken babysitting duty just came with the territory for country life.

It fell to Woody to milk the cow. He had a way with our cow and got the milk out of her quite efficiently. He also entertained us with his antics as he worked. The Sparks family always had a few cats around to keep the mice under control. When one of the cats wandered by as Woody milked, he pointed the cow's tit in the cat's direction and sent a squirt her way. Phil and I loved this and would laugh, hoot, and holler in appreciation.

Mom churned the milk into the best butter you can imagine. All of us appreciated the dairy products generated by our pet cows. Unlike the other animals, the cows tended to live longer, surviving more than just a season or two.

In addition to several black cats, we had a pet dog named Skippy. In contrast to the cats, Skippy sported white fur and loved hanging out with Phil and me. Although we didn't have a lot of free time, we played fetch and other games with Skippy when we could. The dog just liked being in the mix and tagging along as we did our chores.

One time, Skippy disappeared for three or four days. Although not completely uncommon, I got concerned and started looking all over for him. When Skippy returned, I felt overjoyed and showered him with much petting and more than a few kind words. In the next day or so, all of us could tell something was wrong with the dog. Skippy acted crazy, lying on his back and whining in a strange way. Although dogs with rabies often become angry and bite their humans, Skippy merely foamed at the mouth and exhibited strange behavior.

One of our neighbors, Rufford Puckett encountered Skippy up by the road. With the dog foaming at the mouth and acting weird, Rufford knew the cause—and the only cure. He shot our dog. Skippy's passing broke my heart, but I will always remember him as such a good pet. My relationship with Skippy was a highlight of my childhood.

People in our area knew the Sparks kept chickens. Friends, neighbors, and church folks would buy eggs. Once the chickens aged enough that we could discern whether they were male or female, we would sell off all the roosters except one. Word would get out that we had chickens for sale. The going price back then was one dollar per rooster. We would get fifty cents extra if we killed the chicken and dressed it. It wasn't uncommon to get a request for six chickens dressed.

From the youngest age, my parents involved me in killing the chickens. We would extinguish their lives either by axe or by wringing their necks. Dressing the fowl meant boiling some water and dipping the chicken in it for just a minute or two. This scalding bath made it easy to pluck their feathers. Since I became exposed to this process early in life, killing the chickens never bothered me. Being on the production end of the food chain, we each had thick skin about such matters.

There always seemed to be plenty of work for everyone. On Sundays, Phil and I had to haul enough water to the back porch for clothes washing on Monday. Mom and my sisters started on that chore early the next morning. Doing laundry entailed an all-day job. At the farmhouse, Mom and the girls would heat the water in a kettle outside and soak the dirty laundry in a big metal bin with harsh soap. Once it cooled off a little, they might have to scrub any stains on a washboard. Although hauling the water from the creek seemed hard sometimes, I'm pretty sure my sisters got the worst end of that deal.

Around March 15th each year, our family planted potatoes. Mom would cut up a hundred pounds of seed potatoes. Once Phil and I got home from school, we headed out to the garden to plant. This was not my favorite activity. Not only was the weather still a bit chilly at that time of the year, but planting required a different set of motions than I used for other chores around the farm. I always woke up sore during potato planting time. Little did I know how God used that time to prepare me for some of the challenges that lay ahead.

None of the towns near Cow Creek were large in those days. Ravenna boasted a population of 2,400, while nearby Irvine claimed 3,600 souls. Daddy's sister's son managed the Estill County Dairy. Wayne Spicer gave my father a job delivering milk. It felt good to have Daddy home and not having to run to Ohio for construction jobs. Dad began his milk run at four a.m. each day and got off work at three p.m. After the milk deliveries, he would head from Ravenna where the dairy was located over to Irvine. Daddy worked delivering bottled gas until all of his deliveries for the day ended.

Grandpa Sparks owned a farm down the road, but also leased an additional forty acres. He owned a mule or two, which gave him forty acres and a mule. Just a half mile from our house, Grandpa raised a large garden, and tended a few animals beside his mules. I remember being fascinated by his double-shovel plow, allowing him to plow two rows at a time. Every piece of farm equipment that my grandfather used included metal wheels. He would hook up his team of mules and work the ground. At harvest time, Phil and I spent hours forking hay up to the top layer of Grandpa's barn. In those days, we didn't have a motorized hay baler to make things easier. We manually pitched the hay to the top floor. This also built up our muscles.

We saw my maternal Grandpa and Grandma Neal at least once a week. They treated us well, and we looked forward to seeing them. The whole family attended the Ravenna Church of God. Grandpa Sterling worked in the oil fields. Yes, I'm named in honor of my maternal grandfather. He drove a black 1951 Chevy and usually picked us up at Cow Creek to haul us to church. To those who didn't grow up in a Christian family, it's hard to explain how warm and safe it felt to climb into Grandpa Neal's car heading for church. I felt loved and cared for at every level: physical, mental, and spiritual.

Once a year, the residents of Ravenna celebrated Hog Killing Day. Celebrate might be a bit of an exaggeration. Let's just say we observed Hog Killing Day. Everyone in the county killed their hogs at home and brought them to Sam Arthur's house. In his side yard, he had a particularly big sycamore tree. The men and boys would slit the necks of the hogs and pull them upright by throwing chains over the limb of the mammoth sycamore tree. This positioning facilitated butchering the hogs and packing the meat either for the family's use or for sale.

When I was about seven or eight years old, my father decided we needed to kill a hog. It happened on Hog Killing Day. The timing, driven by the outdoor temperature, would allow us to salt and preserve the meat longer through the winter. The chore fell to me. I took a .22 rifle out to the animal pen. Calmly, I laid the barrel between the eyes of the hog and gently pulled the trigger. The animal fell dead immediately, never seeing it coming. I felt no remorse, only pleasure at doing the job my parents asked of me.

In addition to the hen house, we also enjoyed a washhouse/smokehouse structure. This little building included a bench in the back corner. Phil and I would take a couple of hams and salt them down. Then we could leave them out in the smoke house, and the family could eat from them all winter. One of us kids would go out there with a hacksaw. We used it to saw off a certain amount of meat for supper. If a little blue mold had formed on the meat, we just cut it off. Overall, we felt quite blessed at how the Lord and Daddy provided for the family.

Once Phil and I got into our early teens, our adventurous natures led to interesting and fun experiences. Lack of resources never stopped us from having fun. One winter, we hatched a plan to go sledding with our friends Jim and Donnie. Between the four of us, we had one complete, working sled. So, we began scouring around town and eventually found parts of three other sleds. With some scrap lumber and a few nails, everyone made something to ride down the mountain that overlooked Ravenna. We climbed eagerly through five or six inches of new snow to the top, imagining the fun we would have barreling down toward town.

While regular sleds of that era included a steering mechanism to help you turn right or left, not all of us enjoyed that functionality on our jerry-rigged contraptions. Finally, we reached the top of the mountain. Exhilaration pumped through our bodies at the thought of careening down toward town. Like planes heading to battle, we launched one by one down the hill. With no marked course, we zigzagged between trees, stumps, and an occasional good-size rock. Whether for good or bad, our speed built as we flew past bushes and trees.

Phil zoomed ahead with little control of his sled. Like something out of an afterschool cartoon, he spun sideways and ran into a tree part way down the incline. Jim and Donnie reached him, as I fought gravity and lack of control trying to stop my sled. When I got back there, Phil lay motionless on the cold snow. A minute or two passed with no sign of life. At first, none of us said a word.

"Is he dead?" Jim asked.

"Touch him," Donnie said.

Just as we looked at each other, I detected motion out of the corner of my eye. My brother came back to consciousness and looked up through confused eyes.

"Phil, you're okay!" I exclaimed.

"I think so," he mumbled.

Not surprisingly, this minor difficulty didn't put a halt to our fun. We'd dreamed of this day, planned for it, and would not be deterred. Soon, Phil got back on his sled and we all continued down the mountain. At the bottom, we realized that just one trip would not suffice. Soon, we hiked back to the top and did the whole thing over again.

This time, Phil managed to avoid any major tree.

Our fun extended throughout the four seasons. When the weather broke in spring, we cut branches out of a tree and made slingshots. We got a piece of an old tire innertube, cut it up, and made primitive weapons. It was fun to shoot using pebbles and stones.

The four of us liked to play marbles. We usually carried around a pocketful to play against our friends. Jacks represented another popular pastime at recess or when we had extra time after church while the older folks talked.

One of the few widely used toys of the day, a paddle and rubber ball connected by a long piece of rubber string, figured prominently in a major event in my childhood.

My friend, Donnie Watson, got a little bigger after a growth spurt and decided he enjoyed picking on me. After this went on a few times, I'd had enough of it. Walking home from school, Donnie disappeared down into a ditch up ahead of me. I suspected he was planning a sneak attack where as I walked by where he was hiding, he would jump out as he'd done several times before.

Since I saw him disappear from the road ahead, I stopped and grabbed a sizable stick laying on the ground. I slowly approached the place where he had sneaked into the ditch. When he jumped out and yelled at me, I whopped him upside the head. He whined and said something about me not being able to take a joke. I laughed all the way home. His bullying stopped that day. Somehow, beating up on other kids loses its luster when the victim starts fighting back. How could anyone have felt better than I did that day?

The weekend passed and I looked forward to school on Monday. In my mind, everything became right with the world as Donnie got his comeuppance. Just one good wrap on the head, and I made a major impression on him.

The bane of elementary school boys is definitely elementary school girls. True to form, a couple of the girls in our class tattled to the teacher about my "attack" on Donnie. Conveniently, they left out the part about Donnie picking on me in the days leading up to the incident.

"Mrs. Hisle, Sterling and Donnie were fighting on the way home from school on Friday," I overheard one of them say.

Mrs. Hisle grabbed Donnie and paddled him in front of the whole class. Next, she came for me. Compared to my daddy, she had no street cred when it came to paddling. She gave me a couple of whacks on the rear end, but I barely noticed. I smiled from ear to ear thinking about Donnie getting a paddling on top of getting hit in the side of his head. What could be better than putting an end to Donnie's tormenting me than having him get a paddling as well?"

Mrs. Hisle didn't think it funny that I smiled after she meted out her discipline. So, she slapped me on the back with the paddle. I didn't think much about it and honestly, it didn't hurt that much.

A couple of days later, I took my shirt off in front of my mom and she noticed my back.

"Sterling, come over here a minute."

"Sure, Mom, what's the matter?" I asked.

"Your back is all bruised and yellowish. What happened to you?

"Oh, Mrs. Hisle whacked me in the back with the paddle for smiling too much."

When Daddy got home, Mom told him the story and showed him my back. I worried a little that my father might want to paddle me too, but he didn't.

The next day, Daddy went to school, and that's all I heard about it at the time. Years later, he told me what he said to Mrs. Hisle.

"Look, if you ever beat on my kid again, I'm going to come over to your house and whip you and your husband. Don't think I won't." That was indeed the last time Mrs. Hisle paddled or hit me. It's hard to explain how good it feels to have parents who watch out for you.

When Grandpa Neal came to get us for church, all of us enjoyed riding in his car. Church represented a social event, as well as the spiritual benefits. Some weeks, we would go to church on Saturday night, Sunday, and Tuesday night.

Every week, we faithfully attended Sunday School and the main worship service. A solid grounding in faith became one of the biggest gifts my parents gave us during those formative years. I occasionally got the job of watching my baby brother Joe while my parents listened to the adult sermon. My sister, Edith, kept me entertained with her antics.

On Saturday nights, my mother would sometimes be in charge of the church youth program. One of her teaching visual aids included a potato family to illustrate the importance of lessons about life and faith. Mr. Potato, Mrs. Potato, and Baby Potato had starring roles. Mom could make the simplest props entertaining. I laugh now when politically-correct people want to strip Mr. Potato Head and Mrs. Potato Head of their gender. They are potatoes for goodness' sake.

We also formed a little band among the children. I held the cymbals, enthusiastically banging them together. I can remember the pictures of Noah's Ark and other stories which showed us a picture of the God who loved mankind.

Our church, affiliated with the Church of God, Cleveland (TN) Assembly, filled up our lives with love and kept us out of trouble growing up.

One of the main lessons that little church taught me: "Jesus Loves Me, this I know, for the Bible tells me so. Little ones to Him belong. They are weak, but He is strong."

Uncle Burt lead the congregational singing part of the time. What a good example that served for us. Church and faith intertwined everything about our family. To see relatives firmly committed to God meant a lot.

At the age of ten or eleven, I became aware of my sin. Like other members of my family before me, I walked the aisle to the front of the church and knelt at the altar. After repenting and accepting Jesus into my heart, my life changed in ways I couldn't have anticipated. Not long after, I got baptized in the river. On a warm day, the congregation sang, and my pastor baptized me. About 100 to 125 people attended our church, and many of them showed up that day. They sang, "Shall we gather at the river," and the lyrics continue to run through my mind. It's nice to have a point in time to emphasize our commitment to Christ.

Baptism won't save us, but it indicates our willingness to follow the example of Jesus. It also proclaims to the world our allegiance to Christ, a public profession of our inward commitment to God. I never feel embarrassed to be a Christian.

The most frightening thing that happened in my childhood involved our farm and the weather. It started out like any other day, not particularly notable. In the afternoon, the wind started to pick up. As any child knows who plays or does chores outside, when trees start to turn the back of their leaves into the wind, it's about to rain. This helps nourish them, but it also indicates time is growing short if you don't want to get wet.

On this day, the leaves turned over in the wind, and all of us who were outside headed toward the house. As we got to the porch, a tornado dipped down out of the clouds. We ran inside. Prayers went up as the sound of a freight train passed over us.

After the storm, it became very quiet. We filed outside to get a look around.

"Let's see what happened," Mom said, peering out the front door. She opened it, and I followed her out into the yard.

"That old tornado went right down the side of the house," I said.

We all looked at a tree that had been uprooted right next to our home. Then, we walked to the other side of the house. The tornado blew the roof off an out-building. The tornado had split itself in half and missed our house. God protected our family even in the unpredictable weather.

"That's a miracle," my sister exclaimed.

And indeed, it felt like a miracle of God's provision, protecting us from the tornado.

Life continued in that farmhouse for several years. My father's word was his bond, as vendors occasionally offered him credit to make larger purchases. A friend from town would bring Daddy a dump truck load of coal for $8. Many times, we didn't have the cash right at that time. The friend would trust Daddy to make good on the bill.

Dad always paid his bills, which led to another truck-load the next year and a good reputation. People around there trusted my Daddy, which meant goodwill for all of us. Sawmill scraps provided kindling and came in handy for many other purposes around the farm. Wood and coal kept us warm in the house, thanks to our metal stove.

Those days had their share of difficulties, for sure, but it proved to me that anyone can survive the toughest times with hard work and determination. When I see a person begging on the street, no part of me wants to give them a dollar. There are so many jobs available these days. Standing around with a "I'll work for food" sign seems silly. When there are three places on the same block with help wanted signs, why should I give you one of my hard-earned dollars? It goes against the way I was raised. Daddy did whatever it took to support us, even in difficult times. He modeled the right attitude about self-reliance. We prayed, and we worked hard. God provided through the years.

My oldest brother, Ray, eventually joined the Kentucky National Guard. After basic training, he spent one weekend a month on duty. When the Korean War flared up, Ray joined the Army and headed off to fight. I felt proud of him.

All of us looked out for my younger sister, Edith, (her name is pronounced with a short "e" like the man's name Ed and "ith" after it.) As the youngest girl of seven, she probably found her older siblings a bit overbearing at times. In spite of us, she eventually married Roy Puckett, son of our neighbor, Rufford. Cathalene married Junior, Roy's brother. In such a small area, there aren't a lot of choices of who to date or marry.

As a man stands on the threshold of going off to war, his words take on new meaning and seem more important. Before he left, Ray pulled our Dad aside to say something he'd been keeping to himself.

"Look Dad, your wife, my mother is dying from this hard farm life. There are lots of better places she could live, and other places you could work too. Life could be much easier for both of you. Why don't you think about moving the family somewhere else, maybe up north to Ohio where you can get the better paying construction jobs? You know Mom never complains. Even in her condition, she works so hard. Everybody can see the life draining out of her. All this has taken a toll on her body. She's birthed nine children for goodness's sake, even though we lost Gary Lynn, who died after five days, your third girl child, Peggy, died at 12 months old. Then there's the seven of us. All these difficult years have worn Mom out. Please think about moving her somewhere else."

Apparently, Daddy took those words to heart. In 1961, my father sold our farm, and we moved to Ohio.

My brother, Woody, had gotten married the previous year and moved to Dayton when he turned 18 years old. There was no big, formal wedding, but Woody married Darlene and off they went to the Buckeye State. Woody's choice no doubt played into my father's decision also to move north.

*"Lead me, O Lord, in thy righteousness because of mine ene-
mies; make thy way straight before my face"
(Psalm 5:8).*

# 3

It was kind of a strange thing. One day, we were living in a very rural area of Kentucky the next day, we were living in Dayton, Ohio. Just one month into life as a high school freshman, I found myself dropped into a totally different world.

Many of the changes were for the better. We moved from a house with no running water to a two-bedroom apartment on Huffman Avenue in Dayton. My four older siblings had already gone out on their own. That left my parents, myself, Phil, and my youngest brother, Ricky Joe. Although it sounds crowded, our new place had an indoor toilet, a bathtub, a stove, a refrigerator, and running water in the kitchen sink. It felt like a huge upgrade from our accommodations in Kentucky.

We stayed together as a family. That's what really mattered to me. The apartment was a half double. Our living area was upstairs. We climbed the stairs up and down to get into and out of our unit. As a fourteen-year-old, I enjoyed the little market just a block and a half away.

Many of my chores evaporated when we moved. Having modern appliances in the kitchen meant we no longer gardened, but instead bought our food at the grocery store. A refrigerator and stove made life much more convenient. Our new life seemed a long way from hauling water from a backyard well.

Soon, I headed off to Wilbur Wright High School. Although we realized that our speech might be looked down upon by some in Ohio, it didn't bother me. A few of the other kids acted like jerks and made fun of me, but I've never been thin-skinned. I was surprised when my English teacher developed a special interest in getting me to pronounce words "correctly." To me, it felt like taking a foreign language. The other kids in class made jokes, but honestly, their comments slid off like water on a duck's back. I was a big old hillbilly and felt okay about myself. I didn't expect everyone to cater to me or think I was a big deal. That's not how we were raised. Other people were entitled to their opinions.

As a teenager, the new town seemed brimming with opportunity, and I couldn't wait to make some money and get my start in the world. Our family had grown used to doing whatever it takes to make things happen. A few jokes would hardly slow me down.

Three or four months after we moved, we went back home for a visit and stayed at Grandma and Grandpa Neal's house. I loved seeing them again, even though we hadn't been gone very long. We visited around and enjoyed checking up on old friends. Billy Fyke, a former classmate, lived about four miles from our old house at Cow Creek. Not sure if we were wearing a few new clothes or if an Ohio accent started to creep into our speech, but Billy had a profound review of the changes in our family. "You all left here wearing britches, now you come back looking for a place to hang your pants," he told me. Whatever he thought of us, we certainly didn't feel anything resembling prideful at that point. Barely on our feet in our new town, we just enjoyed spending the holidays with relatives.

Back in Ohio after the holidays, a huge snowstorm swept across the area. Schools closed, and Phil and I saw an opportunity. We asked Dad to loan us three dollars each to buy our own snow shovels. Believe it or not, that amount sounded like a whole lot of cash back then. It might have thrown off the family budget if not repaid. Dad forked over the cash, and we promised to pay him back. The young entrepreneurs began scouring the neighborhood.

My brother and I went from house to house drumming up business. We shoveled up one block and down the next, anybody who would pay us. After ten hours of shoveling, we each had earned the princely sum of $3.10. That meant repaying Dad the three dollars we owed and having ten cents profit. For our trouble, we earned enough extra to buy one pack of gum. We didn't lament the arrangement. Now, we each had a shovel and our own small business.

My parents continued their fervent belief in God. We found a Dayton church home right away at the East Fourth Street Church of God. I joined the choir. The group traveled around a bit and sang in area churches. It felt like an adventure to meet new people. After spending my childhood seeing the same relatives and friends every day, how wonderful to have some new people in my life. Soon nature took over, and my focus turned to young women.

The church group served as a great place for fellowship and wholesome fun. Hormones aside, I can remember laughing a lot when we played a game called Poor Old Tom. There is no real point to the game, but one of us would get down on the floor and purr like a kitten. We would go from person to person while they sat in a circle. When it became our turn to act like Tom the Cat, we would meow pitifully. We might rub against someone's leg or just get down on all fours and make cat sounds next to them. The person who served as the object of our cat antics would repeat the phrase, "Poor old Tom." If the person laughed while saying the key phrase, that person must get down on the floor and become Tom for the next round. Although tame by today's standards, we all laughed and enjoyed ourselves with that sort of goofy fun. Such a simple time...

Things moved quickly in Ohio. One of the other church members lived in a half double. For those unfamiliar, that's sort of like a row house, but there are only two of them standing together. This one shared a front porch but had separate front doors. Knowing we lived in a small apartment, the man asked Dad if we would like to rent the other side. Dad quickly accepted, and soon we moved up from a two-bedroom apartment to a townhouse.

The new place had even more amenities, like a little garage where Dad could park his car. We enjoyed a fenced yard. Get this. We even had three bedrooms—two up and one down. It seemed luxurious compared to our first apartment.

In February, we moved to 963 Webster Street in North Dayton. This meant another change of high school for me. Goodbye Wilbur Wright, hello Kiser High School. The change didn't mean a lot to me, but I'm sure it didn't help academically. School wasn't my thing, and I didn't take it seriously.

Soon Phil and I found something that did appeal to us. We heard about a way to make money by selling magazines door to door after school. It felt like my calling. So easy, compared with the chores I'd done growing up on the farm. All I had to do was run up and down specific city blocks and knock on front doors. My pitch highlighted an incredible deal offered by our magazine company.

At the distribution company's office at Fifth and Main in Dayton, we salesmen would get our instructions for the night. Crew Manager Joe Phillips gave us specific streets to troll the houses looking for leads. After we got agreement from the homeowner to try the magazines, Manager Joe would go back to the house, collect the first payment, and get the customer to sign a contract.

"Good afternoon, ma'am. My name is Sterling Sparks. How are you?" Most of the women would answer politely. "I have an incredible offer for you. Do you read?" What red-blooded American woman in the early 1960s would admit to not wanting to read? "I can sell you, not one, but five magazines for just $.25 week." Needless to say, I did well. The profits rolled in, at least compared to what I'd made in Kentucky. Suddenly, I had all the money I needed for snacks and comic books.

The crew manager tried many methods to incentivize us to sell more magazines. One of the perks included a trip to Columbus to see first-run movies!

"If you sell thirty subscriptions this week, I will take you on Saturday to Columbus, and we will watch a movie." This seemed like the opportunity of a lifetime. A movie version of West Side Story had everyone talking. Unfortunately, my parents opposed movies on religious grounds. Although I took my faith seriously, my teenage inquisitive nature found it hard to go along with the danger inherent in motion pictures or the dark places where they were shown.

After working hard and breaking my sales quota, Joe kept his promise and drove a few of us an hour to Columbus. The movie provided more entertainment than I'd enjoyed in my entire life. Youth gangs, singing, dancing, and pretty girls, West Side Story had my mind racing a mile a minute. On the ride home, I dreamed about all the people I'd like to talk to about the movie.

Unfortunately, I had to keep it a secret, even from my brother, Phil, who had moved on to sell magazines for a different distributor. If anyone in my family knew, I could get a stern lecture or Mom's disapproving stare. My big news would have to remain a secret of my new, worldly life as a young businessman.

I kept that job selling magazines until I turned 16. When I reached the age limit for working at a grocery store, I hurried off to A&P to put in my application. They paid big money at A&P, at least compared to selling magazines door-to-door. My natural enthusiasm and penchant for work at a young age won the day. The manager at A&P hired me.

A natural leftie, certain things in life become more complicated. The world is run by right-handed people, and the rest of us must adjust. Running the cash register most of the time, I learned to use my right hand. Prior to modern machines, the manual cash register keys required significant pressure to force them down. Each stroke would physically strike a ribbon onto the roll of paper. Like a small typewriter, the cash register served as a modern miracle.

One wouldn't automatically think about this, but grocery checkout aisles must be oriented for either a right- or left-handed person. Since most people are right-handed, the A&P set up their conveyer belts to deliver the groceries on the cashier's left, leaving their right-hand free to run the cash register. As a natural leftie, I had to learn to strike the cash register keys with my right. Can you imagine learning a new job with your opposite hand? It took a while for me to catch on, and I'm not sure my speed ever approached that of the right-handers.

If the store had few customers, the manager asked me to go into the aisles and "face the shelves." This involved going along and turning all the cans to face out toward the aisle. Back then, we stamped ink on each product to show the price. With no such thing as a UPC symbol, we had to manually set prices on a small device, stamp it on an ink pad, then stamp the bottom of soup cans, for example. One side effect of this system stamping each can required us to change prices whenever the store put an item on sale. We would have to use a product like lighter fluid and a rag to wipe off the ink with the old price. Then we would stamp on the new sale price. Come Monday, we would do the whole thing again for any unsold cans, changing the prices back to the regular cost.

There was a girl back then named Mary Margaret. I took a shine to her and began carrying her books home from school a few times. Awkward and not the most handsome guy just yet, I exuded hormones. Unfortunately, or maybe fortunately, I didn't know what to do with them.

School didn't appeal to me, and I wasn't particularly good at it. My strong suit in a weak academic hand was math. I excelled at all kinds of math, and it felt nice to be good at something. My other favorite subjects included wood shop and metal shop. Perhaps you've noticed a theme by this point. The direction of my life would not involve a lot of formal education, though making money and having my own business sounded great. With a steady job at the grocery, I eventually dropped out without finishing high school.

To say my teeth looked bad is an understatement. My canine teeth grew enthusiastically in my mouth long before the other teeth had a chance to mature. This gave me the appearance of fangs that were off-putting to many young women. My teeth also proved brittle, breaking off when I was eating. Brushing my teeth hadn't been a big priority in my childhood, which led to substantial decay.

When I was 17, the pain and appearance of my teeth led me to seek the help of a dentist. Through a friend, I came upon the practice of Dr. Codus Poaty, who looked disapprovingly at my teeth. After some poking and prodding in my mouth, he stepped back and stared at me.

"I've been in this business thirty years, and you, Sterling Sparks, have the worst teeth I've ever seen. Here's what I think you should do."

Needless to say, I felt surprised by his assessment. Although it sounded reasonable, his recommendation took a moment or two of reflection: He wanted to pull every one of my teeth and fit me with dentures. I thought for a few minutes, but eventually agreed.

The first day, he pulled nineteen teeth. My mouth swelled substantially. Although I didn't miss work, it took several weeks for the swelling to go down. After six weeks, I came back and Dr. Poaty pulled the rest of my teeth. In all, I went two-and-a-half months without teeth. This meant mainly drinking liquids and eating only soft foods. Before the appointment to actually receive the false teeth, my appetite got the best of me. I tried to eat a steak meal the Friday before I was to get my new dentures on Monday. It took a while to get the steak cut up in small enough pieces so I could gum it into submission.

The whole enterprise with my teeth worked wonders. Once I got dentures, I drew much more attention from the young ladies. People started to notice me as my overall appearance improved. I can't remember if I had to borrow some of the money from my older brother, but I eventually paid off all the dental work. Suddenly, my mouth caught up to my attitude, and the women of the Miami Valley became more attentive to my charms.

Available to work fulltime, I gave notice at A&P, which only had part-time work. The IGA hired me to take care of their bottle room. Back in that era, glass bottles required a deposit. The grocery might charge $1.39 for a six-pack of Coca-Cola, but the customer could get five cents per bottle back when they returned the empties.

When customers brought their bottles back for the deposit money, they would set them in a rack by the cashier. My job entailed retrieving the bottles from the racks and bringing them upstairs to the bottle room.

Imagine this massive room upstairs from the grocery with bottles of all shapes and sizes. The Bottle Man (me) would sort the empties by company, brand, and size. There might have been ten companies with ten or twenty different types of soda each. I had to get all the bottles into the right stacks for each soda distributor. Their representative would bring in new stock and take away the empty bottles to be washed and reused at the bottling plant.

The bottle room doubled as the cloak room for the employees. The time clock hung on a wall near the door. People who worked at the store came upstairs, clocked in, and hung up their coats. Some of the nicer folks might stop to talk a few minutes before they clocked in.

One day, I got to work and began going through the ritual of hauling the empty bottles up to the bottle room. After I'd been there several hours, a manager popped his head in and asked me to come with him. Not unprecedented, but this type of interruption by a manager didn't happen every day.

"Sterling, I need to ask you some difficult questions," he said.

"Okay, how can I help?" I asked.

"Do you ever fool with the coats up there in the bottle room?" he asked.

"What? Of course not."

"Well, let me tell you what happened. One of our male employees claims he left his wallet in his coat pocket. After working his shift, he got his coat and went outside to where he'd parked. He found his billfold lying by the side of his car with all the money missing. He believes you may have stolen his money." The manager looked me square in the eyes.

"No way." I said resolutely. The accusation floored me. "No way did I take that money!"

The manager excused himself, leaving me to sit in his office praying. It certainly seemed this man intended to fire me over something I didn't do.

A few minutes later, two police detectives walked into the office. After introducing themselves, they began aggressively questioning me.

"Look, you might as well admit what happened," the older cop said.

"We know you did it," the younger one chimed in. "This whole thing doesn't need to be a big deal. You will be fired, but there's no jail time for petty theft like this. Maybe you will have to pay a fine."

"Forget it," I said. "I didn't do this. I'm not admitting nothing!"

After we each repeated ourselves several times, the detectives offered me the opportunity to take a lie detector test. Of course, I jumped at the chance. Although nervous, I trusted that God would help me clear my name. The test showed I knew nothing about the stolen wallet, vindicating me. I worked my shift the next morning, and the whole thing blew over.

More than likely, my coworker lost his billfold as he got out of his car that day. Someone came along and relieved him of the money inside. They left the billfold for my coworker to find. Jumping to conclusions, the victim accused me because I worked in the same large room with his coat. I continued in my role for several more months.

My time at the grocery served its purpose, funding my first car and insurance. With plenty of walking around money, I felt great about life.

When I turned 18, I answered a job announcement for McCall's—a major magazine at the time. They not only printed their own publications, but many other then-famous magazines, including Reader's Digest. Even after the substantial difficulty of some of my previous farm chores, McCall's required a whole new level of toughness.

The press room where I worked literally printed the pages of the magazines. At that time, they used 600-degree ovens to bake on the color ink. Pages of the magazines raced through an oven with flames on each side of the paper roll. The ovens dried the ink super-fast without burning the paper. I was fascinated to watch the magazines getting printed. After the pages spooled out of one end, large machines cut them into magazine-size publications.

My first role there required brawn and a high tolerance for pain, at least starting out. I worked as a jogger on Leaf Magazine. Jogging books involved catching the finished magazines as they flew out of the machines. Picture magazines flew out of the cutting machine at regular intervals. As the number of magazines in each arm reached critical mass, the jobber would slip them onto carts with shelves—so many per shelf.

If you've ever had a paper cut, you understand the primary job hazard of the jogger. The magazines tore up the insides of my arms as one magazine after the other slid into place. Those first few days, my arms quickly became bloody and cut up. On the first night, I got so far behind with the magazines flying out at me, many more ended up on the floor than I caught. It took a team of five people to help me catch up and preserve the time schedule for the production run. The McCall's work tested me, but I'd learned to stick with even the most difficult tasks. Quitting wasn't in the Sparks family vocabulary.

Over the next weeks, my arms turned leathery as my body adjusted to the grueling work. As I figured it out and grew physically stronger, I could catch four loads of books instead of the usual two loads. I'd stack them on skids and push them down the aisle with a hand jack. After I got really good at it, I could make the run down the aisle, stop for a drink of water, and get back to my post with time to spare before the next batch of books came spitting out.

Life was far from all work and no play at this point. In

some ways, it felt great to have considerable spending money. I bought a black '57 Chevy 210, with red-and-white rolling pleated interior. Working second shift, I got off around midnight. I'd jump in my Chevy and head to Frisch's Big Boy on Keowee Street. It didn't close until 2:30 a.m. The car hops would come out and take my order. The women wore red uniforms that said Frisch's with black pants and a little hat. A few minutes later, I'd have a great-tasting burger and fries. A waitress named Marie caught my eye. I loved to flirt with her from behind the wheel of my Chevy. She had red hair and seemed a little older than me.

One of the most embarrassing moments of my life came about at this time. I was hurrying to get to church to meet my family. My car had a leaky radiator, and I'd spent my last $20 on anti-freeze. After stopping at the auto parts store to buy more anti-freeze, I found myself running late for church and going quite a bit faster than the speed limit. Red lights flashing behind my black Chevy came as no surprise. That car served as a police magnet.

"Where are you heading?" the police officer asked.

"Just heading to church," I replied truthfully.

"I see you have a Kentucky license," the lawman said.

Then a dumb idea came to mind. "Oh, Officer, I'm just visiting here trying to find a job." The lie escaped my lips faster than I could think about it.

"Is that so?" he asked. "Then I have somewhere you need to go with me."

Next thing I knew, the officer escorted me to the nearest police station where the staff entertained me. Unfortunately, my only choice seemed to be calling my father at church. I can just imagine the look on his face when someone interrupted the worship service to tell him Sterling is over at the jail. Daddy drove over to the police station and brought me $20 to put up bond.

"Let's get you out of here before you say something else stupid and get the whole family thrown in jail." His words stung, but he was right.

As the weeks turned into months, I decided to trade in the Chevy for a Chrysler with a big motor. I loved the power of the 1964 Chrysler Indiana State Patrol Car (decommissioned) with a 383 motor and a three-quarter race cam. The car included a push-button dashboard which added to the mystique of that model.

I tried to disguise the former law enforcement vehicle, painting it a custom color and adding chrome strips to each side. The old Chryslers had massive motors, but the company apparently didn't care much about how it looked. It irked me when anyone saw through my car's disguise and said something like, "Isn't that one of those old Indiana State Police cars?"

Out and about, I met a guy driving a 1964 Pontiac GTO with three deuces (three, two-barrel carburetors), which gave the engine more power. The GTO guy bragged about his car so much, I felt compelled to defend the honor of my Chrysler. I bet him $5 that I could beat him by a quarter mile if we raced. This young man seemed more of a hot dog than someone who could dole out the mustard, so he naturally agreed to race me. We made our way to a particularly broad but deserted street. When the starter gave the signal, the GTO sat in one spot and spun its wheels. I ate him up with raw power and tires that gripped the road. As a cheeky 19-year-old, an occasional street race seemed a good way to blow off steam.

Eventually, I got promoted from jogger to inker at McCall's. On the press where they printed Reader's Digest (RD), industrial stairs lead up three stories high. It took seventeen colors of ink to print RD. As an ink man, my job involved running up and down the three flights of stairs to put the correct color ink in the right wells. It required cardiovascular fitness, but also enough strength to haul huge plastic buckets of ink.

No matter how hard a job becomes, our family knew no such thing as quit in those days. Sometimes, I'd work twelve-hour-days, seven days a week. I worked at McCall's from August 1965 until May 1968 when life suddenly took a dangerous turn. My number came up, and I got my draft notice.

A few months earlier, our choir visited a church near Vandalia. I met a young woman named Faye, who was quite attractive. She had moved up north from Tennessee, along with her sister and brother-in-law. Faye and I went out a couple times, but I didn't immediately see us a good match. She seemed much too spiritual for my youthful self. I had romance on my mind, and all she wanted to talk about was church and God. Our chances of developing a relationship didn't look promising to me. When I left for the Army, Faye said she would write to me.

I went into Army basic training from May to August 1968. At Fort Lewis, Washington, I sailed through basic training, which seemed less physically taxing than some of the jobs I'd held at McCall's. After basic, my next stop involved Advanced Individual Training (AIT) at Fort Belvoir, Virginia. I learned how to become a generator repairman. After the training course and thirty days of leave, I left for Vietnam on October 25, 1968. This day will always hold significance as I left a cocky teen and returned a more introspective man.

The whole experience of traveling to Southeast Asia burnt memories into my mind that remain vivid all these years later. Our squad flew from Oakland (California) Air Force Base on a converted civilian plane. Attractive stewardesses offered us drinks, food—anything our hearts desired. Like sheep to the slaughter, we suspected the next days of our lives might hold dangerous surprises. Outwardly, we tried to act calm.

Upon landing in Hawaii, our plane blew a tire, skidding a bit. I hoped it wasn't an omen of things to come. On military time, they own you twenty-four hours a day. No need to be in too big of a hurry to get to Vietnam. We were stuck in an island paradise until the tire got fixed. My fellow travelers and I watched as the beautiful people walked by in the Hawaiian airport, most of them heading to or from vacations. It felt surreal to be sitting there among a plane full of soldiers heading off to war while families, couples, and business people strolled by, seemingly without a care in the world.

A few hours later, we continued to the Philippines. After a short stopover, the same plane flew to Vietnam. Most of us hadn't slept much, and the long flight caused a mix of apprehension and exhaustion.

When our plane came in over Bien Hoa AFB, the flight attendants informed us that the pilots would be turning out the lights for our approach. It got quiet as the cabin went dark. Even on these outer reaches of the war zone, we entertained the possibility the enemy might try to shoot down our aircraft.

The plane seemed to hit the ground with a thud. Instantly, a bunch of wet-behind-the-ears selective volunteers became G.I.s on the ground in Vietnam. My heart raced as soldiers with flashlights hurried us from the plane to buses riddled with bullet holes.

The old bus bounced and rolled along rough, muddy trails until we arrived at base camp about 4:30 a.m. We unloaded from the bus and immediately received our "orientation" lecture.

"If Charlie Cong calls us up and tells us they are going to bomb us, we will be sure to let you know," said a sergeant who'd been in country for a while. "Otherwise, if you hear incoming shells, cover yourself in a mattress and roll yourself up. By the way, Charlie never calls ahead, or at least he hasn't since I've been here."

In the coming weeks, I learned the difference between growing up poor in the Kentucky hill country and growing up poor in Vietnam. There is no comparison. Starving was a very real thing in 1970s Vietnam. The political infighting between the U.S.-backed South and the Chinese-supported North led to much hardship for the people living out in the jungles of the war-torn nation. I was assigned to a company at Long Thang North in the 210 Combat Aviation Battalion. We had seven trucks and only two of them were working the day I arrived. Five needed water pumps. This became my first challenge. With a fellow soldier, we headed into the countryside to see what we could find. I traded with people locally, securing three working water pumps on the first day. After two more trips, I had all five water pumps. Within the first week, I had all seven trucks up and running.

Battalions are made up of Companies. After reporting to Battalion HQ, each soldier found our homes away from home in one of the Companies scattered throughout the region. We flew to our assigned units in choppers with no doors. I kind of enjoyed the experience. It seemed like a new adventure the first time. The upside of this arrangement was I could see everything out the side of the chopper. The downside? The enemy found it a lot easier to shoot people in a helicopter with no doors.

I was a Private First Class (PFC) E-3 when I arrived in country, but my assigned company already had a generator man.

"Sparks, can you type?" someone asked.

"Sure," I said. "They taught me in high school."

So, they put me in the personnel unit. Remember that this is long before personal computers. We typed everything on old-school typewriters. Forms had carbon paper between the sheets of regular paper. If we made a mistake, it meant re-typing the entire document. I typed letters, and organized and processed personnel files for people transferring in and out. I became close with a Captain whose sense of humor seemed to gel with mine. We laughed a bunch, and he made the time pass faster.

During my almost-twelve months in Vietnam, Faye wrote me letters every so often. She talked about church, life in Dayton, and anything else she could think of, I suppose. My letters were probably cryptic and not particularly newsy. The Commanding Officer cautioned us about revealing too much about where we were and what we were doing. All the same, it felt good to have folks back in the United States that remembered me and cared about my well-being.

When he had just a few days left in country, my Captain friend was flying back from an assignment. His plane last showed up on radar flying at 4,000 feet above the terrain heading toward a 6,000-foot-high mountain. The flight boss never heard from the crew again. As the personnel guy, I had to write the report explaining the circumstances. I knew the man well, and now he had died just before the end of his tour in Vietnam. We were friends, and his loss represented a bad situation for sure. How hard I found it to manually type my friend's report, knowing each mistake would mean reliving the words one more time.

On my last trip in country, several of us had already turned in our weapons. We headed into the city when our plane encountered hostile fire. It felt like the irony zone. Could something happen to me so close to my time to leave Vietnam, after surviving in one piece for the better part of a year? My mind raced back to the report I'd written about my Captain friend. We circled the city for half an hour hoping the enemy would lose track of us. It worked.

After eleven months and twenty-five days in country, I left Vietnam and tried hard not to look back.

When I answered a draft notice as a young adult, I didn't think about politics. The morality of the war felt irrelevant. The protests back home didn't affect me any. I went over to where I was called, did my duty, and came home. That's what men do.

We lost my first cousin Patsy Denham's husband, Jimmy, during my time in basic training. He got killed in action. Growing up, I heard stories about two of my uncles who served in World War II. They both made it back alive. I assumed, as a red-blooded American, each of us should do our part when the time came.

Once back in the states, I spent my last six months of active duty stationed at Fort Knox, Kentucky. One day, we heard that Ford Motor Company, in cooperation with the Army, was interviewing guys for mechanic school in Louisville. They rightly figured that after leaving the service, some of us might want to become trained mechanics to work at Ford dealerships.

I went to the base library to sign up.

"Sparks, don't waste your time," the officer in charge bellowed. "There are already seventy names on the list to be interviewed. They are only going to take twenty-five soldiers for the school."

"Where's the list?" I asked.

Confidence was not a problem for me. I'd survived Vietnam. An interview for mechanic school and a well-paying potential occupation seemed like a minor barrier. I became interviewee number seventy-one. When I entered the room for my interview, a man in a white shirt and tie greeted me.

"Good afternoon. Sit down over here. Mr. Sparks, why should I choose you for my school?" he asked abruptly.

"I plan to be a mechanic, whether you choose me for your school or not. I love everything about cars and trucks, and already know a few things about them. In Vietnam, I fixed the water pumps on five trucks before I had been there a week."

The interview went on a while longer, but I think my answer to the first question got me into the school.

Five days a week, the Army bused me back and forth from Fort Knox to Ford Mechanics School in Louisville. I used those mechanic skills for the rest of my time in the Army and beyond.

*"Preserve me, O God: for in thee do I put my trust"*
*(Psalm 16:1).*

# 4

One of life's important lessons: all things good and bad eventually end. My time in Vietnam included many highs and lows. The fellowship with other soldiers and defending my country represented the best part of the experience. Losing a friend and living with fear as incoming shells exploded nearby made a lasting impression on the negative end of the scale. Back home in Ohio in May 1970, my fulltime service had ended, and I went back to work at McCall's. While I figured out what was next, I lived with my parents and paid rent.

At this point, I headed back to church and renewed acquaintances with Faye. Prior to leaving, I'd only gone out with her a couple of times, though I saw her at church more regularly. Now we knew each other a bit better because of trading letters from Vietnam and later from Fort Knox.

A young man looking to begin the next stage of life and a young woman looking for a husband, we naturally fell together as a couple and began dating more seriously. Wedding bells rang later in 1970, and I traded in my bachelor card for a wedding certificate.

Neither of us knew a lot about finances. Having started life in the poor, rural South, the last thing I wanted to do was get into a lot of debt. At first, we rented a mobile home. Unfortunately, the people we rented from couldn't afford to make any repairs. Trust me, it needed some love just to remain habitable. Faye and I decided to buy it and fix it up. We paid the princely sum of $1,100. Both of us owed on our cars and, all told, we found ourselves in debt to the tune of $3,500.

As it always has been to adversity, my reaction became to work harder. At McCall's, the hourly wage of $4.99 seemed like a sizable amount at the time. Not long into our marriage in February of 1971, my manager pulled me aside.

"Sterling, did you hear?"

"Hear what?" I asked.

"They are closing down the pattern division. That part of McCall's is moving to Manhattan, Kansas."

"Oh, they've been talking about that the whole time I've worked here."

Despite my confident attitude, we received notice that our employment would end in ninety days. They couched it in terms of a lay-off. Whatever they called it, we were all out of work just three months later.

The next day, I marched down to the unemployment office. When you filed back then, the clerk gave you 3x5 index cards describing various jobs available throughout the area. Ohio had rules requiring laid off workers to apply for so many jobs per week to remain qualified for the small unemployment checks. I couldn't have cared less about the rules—I applied for every kind of job I could pronounce, whether or not the duties sounded familiar.

In three weeks, I got a job offer from Wright-Patterson Air Force Base Hospital. In the letter offering me the job, they made it clear the position was temporary, not to exceed 90 days. The pay was much lower than McCall's, just $2.97/hour. We were hired as civilian employees to support the food-service operation. I washed dishes, helped in the kitchen, and did whatever they told me. Every three months, they extended my employment for another ninety days until I'd been there a year.

Faye also worked. We eventually sold the trailer, making a few dollars thanks to the improvements we made. This whetted my appetite for real estate as a way to make extra money.

After a year working at the hospital, I tried my hand at selling cars for Frank Z. Chevrolet. As a new car salesman and beginner, they had all kinds of rules regarding when and where we could talk to customers. They probably didn't want us interfering with the experienced guys out on the showroom floor. Our training included not just sales, but the process for manually writing up orders and information about the various makes and models of cars. Since I love cars, it felt like a good fit for me to sell them.

On the sixth day of my second week, I thought about how to find prospects if I wasn't allowed on the showroom floor. During the day, I walked through the service area to look at some new cars parked out back. Striking up a conversation with a man waiting for his car, my instincts proved deadly accurate about prospecting him.

"Sir, are you waiting for your car?"

"Yes, my car is getting a body shop estimate," he said.

"Do you work in the area?" I asked.

"Yes, I work over at the University of Dayton."

"Are you a custodian?" I thought I would try to butter him up, not referring to his position as a janitor. His clothing looked quite casual.

"Actually, I'm a professor. I teach economics there," he replied.

Although embarrassed, I persevered. Despite my initial gaff, he eventually agreed to a test drive, which led to my first sale.

Proud that I'd managed to sell a car without even having access to the sales floor to find leads, I marched into the Sales Manager, Alan Bestco, and presented the deal. Instead of congratulating me or even acting happy that I'd sold a car, he said, "I will expect you to sell two tomorrow."

His attitude didn't improve in coming days. Before long, it became obvious that I wouldn't be happy working there for long. With many of my own prayers and those of my wife, God led me to another opportunity.

At East Fourth Street Church of God, we knew a man named Kenny Isham. He worked as a manager at Tastee Bread, a brand of the American Baking Company. He let me know they had an opening, and I jumped at the opportunity to leave Frank Z. My new job included running bread routes to several of the local grocery stores. Although not complex, I enjoyed being out running around, and I stuck with it throughout the summer of 1972.

One of the most exciting things that ever happened to me was when Faye and I learned she was expecting. If all went well, we would have our first child later that year. While certainly a major milestone for any couple, this ushered in a new way of thinking for me and probably for her as well. She wanted to experience everything about motherhood. After the morning sickness subsided, we settled into the waiting game. It rightly felt like the dawn of a new phase of life.

In September, a letter floated into our mailbox with the potential to significantly change everything. The Army invited me to apply for a job in Huntington, West Virginia. Sensing a significant opportunity, I talked to Faye and made an appointment for the following Saturday. Faye rode along with me from Dayton, a beautiful three-hour drive as the leaves began to turn colors.

The position would require me to go on active duty with the Army Reserves. Most reservists only train one weekend a month besides their annual deployment of a couple of weeks. This job entailed working five days a week, though not Monday through Friday. I would be doing maintenance on Army vehicles used for reserve weekend drills. I liked the idea of the job because it would allow me to use my mechanic skills, and I would get paid more than I was making on the bread truck. Perhaps it might offer a career path to a higher level with Army benefits.

My interview with the military officer who ran the motor pool lasted almost ninety minutes. When we parted, he offered me the job, and I gladly accepted. Now, Faye and I had a major challenge: moving while she was pregnant.

At first, I rented a room at a rooming house in Huntington. I'd work through the week and head home on Friday afternoon. After spending the weekend with Faye, I drove back to Huntington on Sunday night. The separation must have been particularly difficult for Faye with a little life growing inside her. However, the work suited me, and the days flew by.

In mid-November, Faye and I found a house in Chesapeake, Ohio, just across the river from my work in Huntington. We rented out our home in Dayton, packed up a U-Haul truck, and moved that weekend. I showed up for work on Monday like nothing had happened. Faye and I both liked Chesapeake, though Faye had her hands full settling into the house and getting things put away while becoming increasingly great with child.

One surprising bonus during our time there was my Uncle Bert Neal pastored a church nearby. It felt wonderful to see him again and have a small piece of home (Kentucky) so near to us.

That January, at 4 a.m. one morning, Faye woke me up, telling me her water broke. We took my '67 Chevy over the bridge to the hospital. Candy Sparks made her arrival on January 20, 1973, at the Campbell County Hospital in Huntington, West Virginia. The prettiest blue-eyed little girl ever, I fell in love with our baby. All felt right with the world.

In April 1973, Faye and I brought Candy home to Dayton to visit my parents and Faye's sister and brother-in-law. Pauline and Gene helped raise Faye through her teens. One of twelve children and a twin, family was as important to Faye as to me. Everyone fawned over our new baby, and we had an enjoyable visit.

While visiting at my parent's house, I took the short drive over to the Army reserve unit in Fairborn, Ohio. As I hoped, they had a job opening doing auto mechanic work, very similar to my current job in West Virginia. I applied, and it was an easy move back to Dayton, having barely gotten our start in Chesapeake. Fortunately, we were able to sell our house in Ohio and make the tidy sum of $2,300 in just that short six-month span. Again, I saw the power of investing in real estate.

When Faye and I had moved away from Dayton to Chesapeake, we rented out our house to people we considered friends. Our view of them changed after we announced our decision to move back so soon. They did not appreciate being told that we now planned to return to Dayton and wanted our house back.

Apparently quite angry with us, they kicked holes in the walls and did some other damage. It didn't deter me for long. I patched the walls, and soon Faye, Candy, and I moved back in, happily living near family once again.

Faye returned to the factory where she previously worked. I bought a couple of apartment buildings and spent my spare time fixing them up and managing them.

I'd like to say that we lived happily ever after, but life didn't work out that way. Just a few months after we returned to Dayton, I came home to discover that Faye had moved out of our bedroom to a room upstairs. Her decision really bothered me.

My first thought led me to call our pastor.

"Pastor Waggett, this is Sterling Sparks. I have a real big problem," I said.

"Hello Sterling, what's the trouble?"

"It's Faye. You will never believe what that woman has done."

"What's that, Sterling?"

"She done moved clean out of our bedroom and took up living in the bedroom upstairs."

"What do you think is the problem?" Pastor Waggett asked.

"She wants to have another baby right away, and I'm not

so sure. Look, I grew up poor. My daddy did good by us, but it involved struggling all the time. I'd like to just have the one baby right now and give Candy a much better life than I had. We can provide our daughter everything she dreams of."

"I understand," he said. "Look, there are a few things going on here. Couples need to compromise, but having more children is a big decision. You must decide together about more children. Lots of women experience the feelings that Faye is having right now. While they are getting married and then expecting, everyone is paying a lot of attention to them. They are the center of attention. You were probably pampering her and taking care of her. Once she had the baby, all that attention switches over to the child. The grandparents, relatives, and friends, everyone goes ape over the baby. Perhaps even you act more excited about seeing the baby than seeing Faye. It's easy for young mothers to feel overlooked, even fall into depression. Then, it's common for them to get the idea that having another baby will make them feel better."

I thought long and hard about what Brother Waggett had to say. He suggested I come home from work and march right up the stairs and get into bed with Faye, which I did. At least temporarily, this tactic worked. We shared the bed, and daily life returned to normal.

We still had "discussions" about more children, but I wasn't going to give in quickly on that issue. She felt the same.

Work went well, and I enjoyed the guys at the motor pool. The lifestyle of working until three and then heading out seemed ideal. When I left work one day, little did I know what lay ahead. In this life, we need to be ready for anything.

Traveling on I-70 near the New Carlisle exit, I came upon an accident. With dust still in the air, a few cars had pulled to the side of the highway. I got out of my pick-up truck and felt an urgency. I ran toward a semi that had been pulling a flatbed. The overturned flatbed and its load spilled out on the roadside couldn't hide a bright orange glow around the cab of the truck.

"We tried to get him out, but we couldn't," yelled one of two men running in the opposite direction from me.

As I got closer to the truck cab, I heard a blood curdling scream. Someone cried out for help. I jumped on the step of the cab, but the door would not budge. About that time, another man came along and jumped up there with me.

The door felt hot and the whole scene emanated heat and light. The door's lock had been sprung in the accident, but the man inside desperately needed to get out. Otherwise, he would burn to death in front of us. The other good Samaritan and I pulled on the door and the handle as hard as we could. A quick prayer may have made all the difference. With seeming superhuman strength, the two of us managed to unwedge the door and open it.

The scene inside the truck could have been terrifying if we had taken time to think.

"Get me out of here," the driver yelled.

The bone from this man's broken leg protruded from the skin. A substantial amount of blood soaked his pants. We pulled the man out as the flames grew brighter around us. Carrying the trucker to safety on the nearby hillside, we looked back to see and hear the truck cab explode. A minute or two later and the man would have died in his truck, possibly injuring his would-be rescuers.

Before we could think of doing anything else to help the man, a Box 21 ambulance showed up and the paramedics took control. Two news trucks descended on the scene and I spoke with reporters from each station. The next day, no less than four of my friends called to say they saw me being interviewed on television.

Not shaken up, but certainly affected by the excitement, I drove home to Faye. Still covered in the man's blood, I stripped off my clothes and put them directly in the washing machine. A shower helped me come back down to earth. What an exciting mission from God that day! You never know what's going to happen.

Not all of my challenges involved work or such dramatic commute stories. Church in Dayton offered challenges and opportunities. We enjoyed many of the members there, people like Willard Sizemore and his mother. Formerly a drinker, Willard lost his lower legs and feet in an accident at a train yard. He'd been drinking and decided to take a nap under a rail car. He awoke to the horrible realization that the train car was amputating his feet. His disability changed his life. He and his mother became close friends with Faye and me. They were good people.

One Sunday morning in 1976, Danford Settles came to me and explained that the teenagers Sunday School teacher would be absent. She wondered if I could fill in. Although a surprising turn, I felt God wanted me to give it a try. For a couple of years, it became a highlight of my life, preparing the lesson and interacting with the young teenagers. Sometimes, life's challenges are not in the big, dramatic circumstances, but in the regular commitments that strengthen us. Trying to prepare and keep up with those young minds helped me grow in my faith.

*"The heart of the wise teacheth his mouth, and addeth learning to his lips" (Proverbs 16:23).*

# 5

Monday through Friday, I worked on Army trucks. Of the mechanics, I was the only one who had been in the active service. Most were too young to have gone to Vietnam. Although information about Post-Traumatic Stress Disorder (PTSD) was not as widely known then, I later realized that I suffered from a mild case of PTSD. At night, my dreams often turned to nightmares about the unsettling things I'd experienced in the war.

For a time, my job involved servicing the medical unit's trucks. The reservists I worked with didn't have the same war-time experiences. Loud noises had a profound effect on me, but my goal remained to keep my issues to myself. In some ways, it may have been better if I'd taken the time

to talk over my fears with a friend. Instead, I suffered alone
with my anxiety and occasional battle with fear.

I enjoyed my job with the Army Reserve. My buddies
and I worked on a variety of vehicles, including the two
pick-up trucks that were assigned to the shop area. We
used them to run after parts we needed to fix the other
Army vehicles. Each pick-up was painted Army olive-drab
green, very recognizable to anyone who has been in the
service. One day I needed to make a run for parts from
our shop in Fairborn, Ohio, to Springfield, only about
twenty minutes away.

My friend, Earl Martin, had just finished a brake job on
one of the three-quarter-ton pick-up. "Hey, Sterling!" Earl
said. "Do you mind taking this pick-up? I just finished
the brakes, and it needs a test drive."

"Sure, buddy," I answered. "No problem at all."

Earl and I had worked together for years. A regular
guy, he seemed to enjoy my stories, and we got along well.

The trip to Springfield included main roads and high-
ways. The pick-up quickly came up to speed, and the truck
seemed to be handling normally. I loved going for rides
in the middle of the day. It seemed to break up the shift
and make the afternoon pass quicker.

As I traveled on the highway, a driver ahead of me suddenly slammed on his brakes. I had to punch the truck's
brakes pretty hard to keep from rear-ending the person
ahead. The Army pick-up's brakes locked up, and the truck
went a bit sideways. Next, my truck rolled over four times.
I'd never been in an accident like this. The rolling seemed
to go on forever—in slow motion. Finally, my truck came
to a rest upside down in the ditch.

I'd spun four-and-a-half rotations and come to a
stop with my head resting on the ceiling of the truck.

Disoriented, I sat there a few moments before I tried to move. At that moment, my mind went back to a scene of my co-worker filling a pick-up with gasoline just before I left for Springfield. Mildly panicked, I hurried to get oriented and try to figure out what to do next.

The vision of gallons and gallons of gasoline cascading down on my head caused considerable alarm. I unbuckled my seatbelt and crawled out the window of the truck. Except for a scratch on my arm and a little overall soreness, I escaped the accident without serious injury. Praise God!

Back at the shop, I let Earl know the brakes may have been adjusted just a shade too tight, times ten! Since the Uniform Code of Military Justice does not allow soldiers to choke each other, I had to let the whole thing go and forgive Earl.

The motor pool garage provided a relaxed atmosphere most of the time. Trucks would come in based on a maintenance schedule. During the week, we would do the service, oil changes, lubrications, change out ball bearings, etc., in civilian clothes. Mechanics only had to wear our uniforms on our drill weekends.

My role evolved as I moved up the chain of command. Eventually, I became an Acting Sergeant, running the motor pool. As the boss, I did paperwork and assigned the other mechanics to various jobs that came through our shop. The brass promoted me to Staff Sergeant, and eventually I became the Battalion Motor Sergeant, an E7.

My sister, Cathalene, lived at the family's former home back in Kentucky. Each year, Faye and I would travel down there for the family reunion held the first week of June. Those of us who had moved north to Ohio made the trip to Kentucky amid heavy traffic both ways. On Friday nights, the cars streamed south. On Sunday evening, they streamed back on I-75 North—the migratory habits of the transplanted Kentuckians. One could look across to the other side of the divided highway to see only a few cars in comparison. This odd ritual only varied when an accident or construction lane closures slowed traffic on our side of the Interstate.

My two sisters cooked a ton of great food for reunion weekend. The rest of us would bring desserts or side dishes that traveled well. Since our family is rooted in faith and the example Mom and Daddy provided, these gatherings didn't include drinking or a lot of carrying on. We just liked being together, enjoying family times, and letting the children play together. As Mom's life was winding down, I sensed another change for our family. This caused some advance mourning for me. The sense that the good times were ending overshadowed the enjoyment on some of those visits.

While life buzzed along normally at home, Faye and I continued to clash over the subject of more children. As born-again Christians who try to follow the teachings of the Bible, neither of us believed divorce to be an option. We talked with our pastor or others from the church. Some of the couples tried to encourage us. Hours of counseling and many fresh starts left us both tired, but we hung in there for the sake of our beloved daughter Candy.

An E8 job opened up with the Army Reserve Medical Group. I asked Sergeant Estes (who decided who would go to which training courses) to please sign me up. To get the E8 job in the Medical Group, candidates must take medic training. I didn't have the required courses, so it would be impossible for me to get the promotion to E8.

"Let me go to Medic School and learn," I said. "I'd like the chance to get promoted."

"Look, Sparks, don't you think you are getting a little long in the tooth to become a medic?" Sergeant Estes asked. "Besides, who is going run the motor pool while you are off learning to be a medic?"

"That isn't for you to decide," I said, growing increasingly angry at this peer who shouldn't have had an opinion on the subject. "It isn't your job to tell me what I can and can't do."

Apparently, we made enough racket that our superior officer heard the commotion and came out of his office.

"Sergeant Estes, just sign Sergeant Sparks up for Medic training," the Colonel said calmly.

That's all it took. Within days, I left my regular duties and attended medical training for three months. It felt good to be away from my normal job, and it took some of the pressure off Faye and me. Perhaps one of the reasons couples struggle is just boredom with the same old life struggles. A change of venue or job may be just the thing to breathe new life into a tired perspective.

The medic training included a significant amount of learning in a short period of time. I found the studies challenging, but enjoyable overall. After keeping the routine of the motor pool for several years, this offered a chance to meet some new people and expand my capabilities.

As part of the medical training with the Army, my unit assigned me to the Dayton Veterans Administration Hospital. Many soldiers and other military members come to the VA for their healthcare. Upon arrival, they assigned me to an office job since I already had the Human Resources/ Personnel specialty on my Army service record.

Through the week, I again worked regular business hours and enjoyed the office environment there. One young woman in the office treated everyone well, but she kept a deadly secret. Married to a violent man, she was going through a divorce.

On Saturdays, this young lady would interact with the Army Reserve men who trained at the hospital for their monthly weekend service. She and one particular sergeant hit it off. The sergeant worked with me in our group, and I liked him. He proved dependable and proficient at his job.

One Sunday, after I'd worked with the sergeant and this young woman the previous day, neither of them showed up for work. At first, I didn't pay a lot of mind, but certainly wondered what might be going on. About that time, a stranger showed up at our office.

Flashing his credentials, the man said, "Do you know this man?"

I looked at a Xerox copy of the sergeant's Army identification. "Yes, he works with us on the weekend. Is he in any kind of trouble?"

"You might say that. He's dead. I'm with the Montgomery County Coroner's office. We have his body at our facility. His head's blown off with a shotgun, but this I.D. was among his possessions. Apparently, he was having an affair with a young woman from your office."

"That sounds possible," I said.

The detective continued, "The women's husband paced up and down in the hallway outside of her apartment all night. When the guy came out the next morning, the husband shot and killed him. He also shot the woman, but we expect her to live."

Later, I learned that the jealous husband had previously threatened his wife many times. If she ever left him again, he promised he'd kill her. Apparently, he tried to make that happen. Moving out and getting her own apartment didn't squelch her husband's interest in stalking her. Although she recovered from her wounds, sadly, the attack left her blind. Her husband is serving a lengthy sentence in prison for murder.

A week later, the sergeant's family arranged a closed casket funeral. With others from the Army Reserves, I attended the wake and funeral service. When I approached the casket to pay my respects, a man who looked just like the sergeant stood nearby. It turned out he was the sergeant's brother. It was unnerving to see someone at the funeral who looked so much like our deceased friend and colleague.

At the end of the medic school and practicum, I proudly became an Army Medic. My expectation that I'd be immediately promoted to E8 did not materialize. I submitted the paperwork, but nothing happened. Later, I learned that a certain individual held the paperwork at his desk, so my application never came up for consideration. My superiors didn't promote me because the decision-makers never saw my application. Months went by, and I didn't know what was going on.

I diligently reviewed job announcements posted on a bulletin board on our facility. One day, I noticed a bulletin from 83 ARCOM for a warrant officer slot. Interested in that promotion as well, I called the commander who would make the selection. I went for an interview after work on a Wednesday night. When I had answered all of his interview questions, he said, "You've got the job. Just put in the paperwork."

The next day, I went to Columbus and completed the paperwork. Having learned my lesson from the last time, I skipped the battalion individual who pocket-vetoed my previous application. Soon, a notice arrived from ARCOM. The promotion board would meet with me.

Although a bit nervous with the stakes involved, I showed up for the board interview. Across from me sat two colonels and a warrant officer. Apparently, the interview went well. I got my commission in 1986. Just before that time, the Army made a change that established warrant officers as commissioned officers. If the commander of a unit got killed, the warrant officer would be in charge. I received a call from ARCOM. They asked if I felt comfortable leading as the second in command. Of course, my response was a hearty, "Yes, sir!"

"Come up tomorrow, and we will swear you in as a warrant officer."

This felt like a major milestone in my Army Reserve career. I'd thought about this promotion and the additional pay for a long time. Doing everything I could to make myself qualified and ready, it felt satisfying to finally get the rank that had so long seemed just beyond my reach.

Our motor pool unit had plans to deploy to McAlister, Oklahoma, on our annual training expedition. There is a tradition that newly-promoted warrant officers must pay a dollar to the first service member who salutes him.

As God and luck would have it, the very individual who didn't forward my earlier promotion paperwork turned out to be my first salute. After returning his salute, I shook his hand with a folded-up dollar in my hand. He received it with a wry look on his face. His expression said everything and made the accomplishment all the sweeter.

Although at a high point in my career, my marriage to Faye continued to deteriorate.

I got up on Saturday morning and made my way to the kitchen. Faye waited for me with something obviously on her mind.

"Look, I plan to take a little money out of my retirement

and buy a new car," Faye said.

Raiding the retirement account sounded like a very bad idea to me. This one act felt like defiance because we'd talked about saving for the future. My temper began to flare.

"If you take money out for a car, you may want to take a little extra. You will need a place to stay, too." My words were meant to hit home and they did. She went ballistic and the fight ended badly. Months and years of frustration for both of us took their toll. Finally, the unthinkable became an option.

In 1986, we decided to call it quits. This decision wasn't taken lightly. I thought about many things besides my personal unhappiness. I thought about the possibility that we could stay together, and our arguments would escalate. Most of all, my thoughts involved how our divorce might affect our daughter. The time felt right to do something, so I moved out and filed for divorce. The procedure took months, and we saw each other often as I picked up my daughter for weekend custody. I cherished the times with my child, but the stress she endured during this period became undeniable.

As Faye and I saw the effects of the divorce on our daughter, we decided to remarry in 1987 and provide a stable home for Candy. Just a short time after I moved back in, I knew I'd made a terrible mistake. The fighting began anew, and I felt more trapped than ever. We hung on, knowing Candy would graduate from high school in 1991. Day after day, we became more miserable.

The last four years of our marriage included a lot of hiding on my part. Working fulltime during the day at the Army motor pool, I would leave there and stop by the Century 21 office for messages, leads, and updates on properties new to the market. After a quick stop at home and sometimes dinner, I would leave my pick-up and head out in the Cadillac to show houses. In addition to her job, Faye involved herself in Candy's school activities and with the other women from church.

In 1991, I turned forty-five just as Desert Storm began brewing. To fight a full-scale war in the Middle East, the U.S. Army faced tremendous logistics challenges. Our reserve unit began preparations to move vehicles and equipment into position, first in the United States, and then abroad.

One evening, I came home from work feeling the weight of the impending war and the long list of preparations on my work to-do list. Faye and I quickly fell into an argument over something unimportant. The added pressure did nothing for my mental state at the time.

"Look, we are getting ready for a war. Do you get that? Getting ready to deploy, we have more and more things to do every day. If this turns out to be an all-out war, I may go over there and not ever come home. This Saddam Hussein guy is a nut case. He uses chemical weapons on his own people. Who knows what he has cooked up for us?"

"What about our marriage?" Faye asked. "Don't you care about that?"

"This marriage is over," I said. "If I come home from this war, it won't be to live here with you. I can't stand it anymore."

We slept in separate rooms that night. For too long, we'd put off the inevitable out of deference to our daughter, our faith, a million reasons. At this point, none of them seemed to matter anymore. I needed out of the relationship more than any other thing on earth. We could sort out the damage later. One thing seemed of the utmost importance. I just couldn't live the rest of my life in a loveless marriage. Getting free seemed the only important thing.

As soon as my orders came, activating our unit, we drove a lot of heavy equipment in a convoy up to Fort McCoy, Wisconsin. All of our tanker trucks needed to go on a long trip, and this was just the beginning. After putting the vehicles on train cars, my platoon mates and I traveled to New Jersey. We needed to be there to unload everything when it arrived at the end of the line. Next, we loaded the tankers on ships and sent them off to Saudi Arabia. Once all of the material arrived, our unit set up camp thirty-five miles from the Iraqi border.

In addition to our own vehicles, a sergeant from another battalion sergeant major came to our company and asked us to do maintenance on their trucks as well. As a condition of taking on the extra mission, I insisted that he loan us his mechanic to help us take care of his vehicles. He agreed and the deal was struck.

On the first night of our arrangement, I contacted his mechanic and told him what time to report the next day. He said, "I have guard duty tonight until 0400 hours." The sergeant major had assigned the man a shift that ended a few hours before he was to report to the motor pool.

Minutes later, I was on the phone with his boss, who had loaned me this soldier in exchange for doing their maintenance. "Look, it won't work that way. You can't loan me a mechanic and then keep him up all night on guard duty."

He saw the error of his ways and wrote it off as a nice try, I suppose.

One of the challenges of Desert Storm involved the age of the fleet. Our tankers were twenty-year-old trucks.

Supplying the needs of the U.S. troops required sixty-one, 5,000-gallon fuel tankers to keep all the vehicles going. Most of these trucks had not been operating in sandy climates. The desert conditions required a whole different level of maintenance, meaning much more servicing to keep them running.

Our first mission involved following behind the advance force of tanks and helicopters as they entered Kuwait. Until our version of D-Day, our troops would live out in the desert and wait.

Being raised on a farm as a child, I'd grown up with little in the way of comforts and luxury. As long as I could get a cup of instant coffee once in a while and a little sleep, I could handle the heat and oppressive conditions. The kids we took to fight Desert Storm had a totally different frame of reference. They were not used to living in a hot tent, sleeping on a hard cot, and eating much less tasty food than at home. Due to the special reputation of Saddam Hussein, we were advised to wear chemical suits and have our gas masks nearby. Let's just say the entire experience took some getting used to for everyone. Imagine trying to wear a chemical suit in oppressive dessert heat. That's the way it was!

As a warrant officer, I slept in the command tent with a squawking radio nearby. It bleated on and off all night long. At 12:01 a.m. one evening, the radio blared. War would be declared in a few hours. It was go time.

The impending announcement took a toll on one of our unit's inexperienced sergeants. He started pacing back and forth, wringing his hands, and babbling incoherently. Part of my job as the old man of the unit included calming down people like him. God helped me to say the right things to him and others at the right time. Until we are put under extreme stress, no one knows for sure how they will react. It's easy to judge others sitting in our safe, warm homes thousands of miles away from danger. It's another thing to know you are going into battle the next day.

Still behind the demarcation line, my unit fueled up the vehicles as they moved out. One of the sergeants and I needed to go into town to buy additional supplies. I still find the sights in town difficult to describe. At least in the early 1990s, the city where we roamed proved quite an eye-opener. There is no kind of crazy like the insanity we saw there.

On our way back from procuring the needed provisions, a Saudi driver in a truck came hurdling at me, traveling about sixty mph. The narrow road we traveled had been built about four feet off ground level. This helped the road stay above the sand in wind storms. When it became clear that the other driver was not going to swerve out of the way, I had to bail out into the desert.

Our large, supply truck descended with a loud thud, and I was jolted forward out of my seat. When we came to a stop, I knew something bad had happened to my body.

"Are you alright?" the sergeant asked.

"Something snapped in my back," I said.

"Can you move?"

"Not exactly," I said.

The sergeant used the radio and called for help. It took some time to get the Army Ambulance out to us. They carefully loaded me into the back and drove off toward the same Saudi city where we had bought supplies earlier in the day. A commander told me I would be in the hospital at least two weeks. My mind ran through many scenarios.

Apparently the first hospital did not have all the equipment needed, so they loaded me back into the ambulance the next day and took me to a different hospital. After a couple of days there, they flew me to the U.S. Air Base in Germany, where I got the news that I'd broken the L1 and L2 vertebrae. It might be more accurate to say, these vertebrae got crushed in the process. Doubt and fear tried to overwhelm me.

People back home got the news, including Faye and Candy. Prayers went up from many corridors. I credit the considerable number of prayers and God's grace that I wasn't paralyzed or worse. The doctors told me if I'd been thrown backward instead of forward, I probably would have died before they got to me.

Immediately, I tried to assert the iron will that caused me to hang there at McCall's as my arms ached with paper cuts. My plan included getting well quickly and getting right back into the fight. Even when leading our unit, I wore a knife and a gun. It was part of my identity as a soldier. At each hospital, they took my knife and gun away from me for safe keeping. That was the hardest thing. To me, it meant I was not a soldier anymore.

As we left each hospital, I had the same conversation with the nurses upon check out. "Sparks, are you ready to go?" the nurse would ask.

"No, I need my knife and firearm."

You might say I threw a fit each time until they gave in. Eventually, they would send my weapons along with me to the next place.

Back in the States, Washington, DC, became the next stop on my healing journey. My health continued to improve, and I felt confident that life might someday return to something like normal.

After a month or so, I was flown in a DC-10 to the hospital at Wright-Patterson Air Force Base (WPAFB). It was the successor to the same Dayton hospital where I'd worked as a cafeteria employee many years earlier. After more tests and prodding, the doctor at WPAFB Hospital gave it to me straight.

"Look, Sterling, we can do three things. I can operate and replace the damaged vertebrae with new ones. Another choice is to insert steel rods and keep your spine in a rigid position. The third option is just to fuse what's left of your two vertebrae together. Honestly, I can't promise that any of the three operations will leave you in less pain than you are experiencing right now. For each option, I've had patients who experienced significant pain relief and many who have the same amount of pain."

After some thought and prayer, I decided to get by without surgery, at least for the time being. None of the options came with an assurance that the outcome would serve me better than just hanging in and letting my body try to heal itself.

To this day, I'm getting by with just prayer and an occasional over-the-counter pain reliever. God has helped me deal with the damage and the residual pain.

When I was discharged from the hospital, I made my way to the Army Reserve office and applied for disability. Little did I understand the process or the likely outcome. Anyone who serves in the military learns about the positives and negatives of a large bureaucratic organization. If the regulations say to fill out form 27X, you don't argue or procrastinate. It does no good. You just fill out the form and plan on following up to see if the form is processed in a timely manner. We also learn, once all the correct procedures are followed, the squeaky wheel sometimes gets the grease.

I used both lessons throughout the following months

to eventually obtain a determination about my future.

As an officer overseas, I received a housing allowance and food allowance. The day I visited the Reserve office, they immediately eliminated my housing allowance. As for my disability, the Army determined that I qualified for just half of my regular pay.

After fighting for a year using the appeals process, no change was made to the determination. My disability retirement was fixed at thirty percent.

I left the Army Reserves and never looked back. They never increased the percentage rate of my compensation. Still, my pride about having served remains undimmed. I learned what many others have also discovered: veterans don't always get the best deal in exchange for their service. We put our lives and bodies on the line. Some don't come back at all. Others fall victim to injuries in battle or in doing our normal jobs. Soldiering is not a job everyone wants to do, but it's a job every nation needs if it wants to remain free of tyranny.

As promised before I left for Saudi Arabia, I divorced Faye. My injuries didn't change anything. We fought and didn't get along when I was at a hundred percent. How could that possibly improve with me in pain and wondering what I might do for the rest of my life? We sold our house and went our separate ways. It took a toll financially on both of us, but I felt relieved. In my case, the divorce was worth it.

The pain from my Desert Storm injuries didn't immediately or ever completely subside. I learned to manage pain with over-the-counter medication. There I sat: divorced, living in an apartment, and not sure where to go next. It was one of the lowest points of my life.

*"I have gone astray like a lost sheep; seek thy servant; for I do not forget thy commandments" (Isaiah 53:6).*

# 6

Although I knew I didn't want to live with Faye anymore, my mind wasn't settled about remarrying. Spiritually, you could say that my relationship with the Lord slipped into hibernation after Faye and I divorced the second time. No other woman waited in the wings. It wasn't about someone else. I wanted a new life. On the other side of moving out, my only plans included getting my own place, surviving, and parenting our daughter.

I hadn't ruled out dating and trying to find someone eventually, but I wasn't eager to get back on the horse. I like women and always have. I like being in a relationship. My religion at the time warred with my legitimate need for companionship and my desire for physical relations.

The result of the internal conflict: I put God on the back burner and tried not to think about Him most of the time. My life became more about getting past my back problems, finding a job I liked, and buying a house again.

Raised in the church with a praying Mom, there is no way I could erase the need and desire for God. Her words often echoed in my mind.

All during this period, I ran from Him. No matter where I went, God still seemed nearby. Not sure if he is the Hound of Heaven, but He is definitely a Chatty Cathy to backsliders. His voice of love reached out to me over and over.

My reduced pension from the Army paid the bills, but it took a while to find a second career. You may wonder, what about real estate? I'd left that behind too. Things were changing in the real estate industry. The thought of learning a bunch of new technology didn't appeal to me. Younger people brought new attitudes about buying property, and the writing on the wall implied the entire real estate industry might be turned on its head by the Internet. Everything seemed to be getting more complicated and less profitable for the average salesman. A real estate downturn made my decision even easier.

Weeks turned into a couple of years, and I felt lost. Nothing seemed like the right path, and my back pain became a wilderness experience.

A few years after my divorce, I starting dating a few women. It felt foreign to again be on the dating market. I eventually found an attractive woman who seemed right for me. We laughed together and saw each other off and on.

This woman bought a farm in the country. I spent considerable time helping her fix up the property and house. With no full-time employment, it seemed like a worthwhile use of my time. Perhaps she and I would eventually marry and settle down? Who knew?

As the months went by, I began to get hints that she wasn't telling me the whole story. What I didn't know is that the periods when she became unavailable exactly corresponded to a long-term affair she was pursuing with a married doctor. I was the last to know. Somehow, I knew things weren't progressing in the right direction. After some soul searching, I realized that cutting off the relationship looked like the best option.

I needed a job and a new life. As I thought about the end to my military career, my options for non-physical labor all revolved around the auto industry. My love for automobiles made car salesman an obvious choice. One of the dealerships not far from where I lived, Jack Walker, happened to be hiring a new training class of salesmen.

Due to the washout rate, they hired a few people at a time and trained us in a small group. The ones who could swim (sell cars) survived, and the others moved on to their life's work elsewhere. The challenge intrigued me. Since my magazine-selling experience went well as a teen, perhaps car salesman deserved another chance for me.

Not long after I starting working there, the owner's son, Jeff Walker, struck up a conversation.

"Sterling, do you drink coffee?" he asked.

"Very much," I said. "It's one of my favorite things."

"We rent our coffee machine. The supplies come in once a month. Someone has to take the lead in managing the coffee area. The Coffee Lead receives the supplies and keeps track of what we need, stores the coffee in his locker, and makes the first pot in the morning. We also ask the coffee guy to clean occasionally to keep the table looking neat. If you will take care of the coffee area, I won't ask you to chip in the $4 per month that the other salesmen pay to drink coffee."

"Sounds like a deal to me," I said.

For free coffee, the deal sounded like a small price to pay. As the coffee guy, I could make a fresh pot whenever the urge struck me. My locker served as the coffee supply room. Honestly, it seemed like a minor chore while waiting around for customers to show up. Salesmen experience a lot of downtime in the car business. Little did I know the profound impact my coffee-making decision would play on my future.

Our dealership always threw a big end-of-the-year sales promotion event. People like a good sale, and the dealership buzzed with activity. With all the traffic through the showroom, I sold six cars over a couple of days. I felt pretty good about life. My mood no doubt showed it.

On the very last day of 1995, a beautiful lady strolled into the dealership to trade her Pontiac for a new car. Another salesman waited on her. Once she decided on the right car, she sat down at a desk not far from mine. Her salesman bobbed back and forth getting her paperwork and starting the process of sending her home in her new vehicle. I noticed her sitting just a couple of desks down from my cubby hole.

"Would you like anything to drink?" her salesman asked.

"I would love a cup of coffee if you have one," she replied.

Sensing an opportunity to be helpful and to meet this charming beauty, I piped up, "I just made a pot. I will bring her a cup while you get her car ready."

That's how I met Julia. After pouring a coffee and returning to where she sat, I began with small talk. She easily held up her end of the conversation. We found a lot of common ground. She took care of her parents and drove them to a lot of doctor appointments and other places. I did the same for my parents. Both of us were in relationships that seemed to be heading nowhere. We got to talking back and forth and laughing about this and that. She was the oldest child and talked mainly about her family. Obviously, family is a favorite subject for me too.

As the time passed, I wished I could see her again, and she seemed open to the idea. I scribbled down my name and phone number and handed it to her.

"If you want, call me some time," I said trying to be as smooth and casual as possible.

She turned the paper over and began writing something. When she finished, she handed me back the paper. "You call me."

That one simple act only made me even more curious. As a man with traditional values, I liked that she wanted me to take the lead.

Julia and I began dating off and on. Our other relationships fell to the wayside soon after we met. Occasionally, we would get peeved with one another and not call for a few days. After our tempers cooled, one of us would call, and we would go out, starting the cycle all over again. It felt like love, the dance of emotional highs and lows.

About this time, my daughter Candy completed her studies at Ohio State. She planned a graduation party and invited me to come.

"Can I bring Julia?" I asked.

"Of course. I would expect you to bring your girlfriend," Candy said.

"Will your mother be there?"

"Yes, but we are all adults."

With those words, I first confronted the awkwardness of seeing my ex again with another lady in tow. How many times at that graduation party my mind replayed the words "We are all adults"?

Inside, I've never felt completely at home with the role of adult. I don't feel like a grown-up. Now playing the role of an adult feels strange. Although a former soldier, mechanic, and father, there are times I feel more like a teenager playing the adult role. At Candy's graduation party, I had to go through the experience of confronting my fears about seeing Faye. To get to the other side, the only cure rested in attending the party with Julia. Faye and I treated each other in a civil way and put the focus on our daughter, as it should have been. Conversation flowed easily enough, and the energy of Candy and her friends lit up the evening.

A few years after that first meeting, Faye and Julia would meet again in the run up to Candy's wedding. As her parents, both of us wanted and needed to be involved. We loved the opportunity to see our daughter wed someone she loved. I no longer felt nervous about Julia and Faye being at the same event. The last thing Faye or I wanted to do would be to disappoint our little girl on her big day.

On October 18, 1996, my father passed from this life to eternity. My respect for him never diminished. As he and my mother got older, it became a privilege to pick them up at their home and take them on errands, out to restaurants, or any other opportunity to get out of the house. As the middle son, it wasn't out of obligation, but driving them around felt like an opportunity to continue the relationship we built. I wouldn't take anything for the experience of these precious times with them individually or as a couple. Dad was 81 when he died, which seemed like a nice long life back then. (Now it seems young.)

At the funeral, my mind wandered to wonderful times we had together, just the two of us. As he got older, Daddy enjoyed going to flea markets. In Ohio and Kentucky, flea markets were a major source of fun and minor source of income for many people. We would browse through the acres of booths and tables, looking for an underpriced item. During one outing to a Dayton flea market, Daddy came upon an older man who looked to be near his age.

"What's the least you will take for that axe?" Daddy asked. This represented my father's opening line. He hoped to get a baseline to start the negotiation.

"The least I will take is $14.50," the man answered.

"Okay, I will buy it for $14," Daddy replied, trying to shave 50 cents off the price.

Unfortunately, he'd encountered a man who said what he meant and didn't intend to go any lower in price.

"No, it doesn't work like that. I need $14.50. That's what I said, and that's what I mean."

Daddy turned to me and asked in a breathy whisper. "Sterling, should I take the deal? I can get $17 or so for the axe at a garage sale."

"This is your thing, Daddy. Do as you want to do. If you can make money on that axe, do what you think is right," I said.

We walked away with the axe, just $14.50 lighter in the wallet.

Interspersed with the buying and selling, Daddy taught me a lot about life at those flea markets. My admiration for him only grew in his later years.

My recollections at the funeral continued as the preacher waxed eloquent about my father. I thought about Dad's conversation with a younger buyer who came to one of

Daddy's garage sales. This young buyer asked, "Can you guarantee this hammer will never break?'

Daddy smiled and said, "If you'll take the hammer home and leave it up on your shelf, I promise you it will never break."

That's the risk we all face with living and loving. It hurts to lose someone you love. As prominent a role in my life as my father played, his passing cut deep. That's the cost of loving with your whole heart.

Although he lived a long time, my respect for Daddy never diminished. He and Mom raised seven kids with very little money, particularly during our time in Kentucky. Through hard work and with a little ingenuity, our family got along better than most. We always felt loved and taken care of in a world where many struggled through the poverty of those days.

My oldest brother, Ray, attended Daddy's funeral, of course. He came up from his home in Murfreesboro, Tennessee. I thought about the fun times taking Mom and Daddy to visit Ray's house once a year. They loved spending time with family, and Ray in particular.

Of course, Daddy wanted to visit flea markets in Tennessee too. Perhaps there are differences in Tennessee second-hand items. My father liked fooling with stuff, and restoring old treasures gave him something worthwhile to do. He might clean up a hammer, put a new handle on it, and make 50 cents on the whole exchange. Ray understood, just as I did, that rehabilitating random items gave Daddy satisfaction and kept him busy.

After the funeral ended, most of the mourners took time to eat a meal with us at the church. We surrounded Mom with the love she always gave to us so freely. Mom handled Dad's passing really well. She probably shared our gratitude that he stayed alive so long after receiving an artificial heart valve in 1972. The fact that he lived twenty-six more productive years felt like a sincere blessing.

*"Wherefore seeing we also are compassed about with so great a cloud of witnesses, let us lay aside every weight, and the sin which doth so easily beset us, and let us run with patience the race that is set before us" (Hebrews 12:1).*

# 7

To understand my relationship with Julia, you need some background about my religious beliefs. For most of the time Faye and I were married, we attended the Church of God of Prophecy. A fundamentalist denomination, one of their core beliefs (at least in those days) labeled divorce evil and remarriage a sin. If one divorced, the church taught us that person must not marry again as long as their first spouse lived. Those teachings played in the back of my mind like a cassette tape. If I married another woman, it would be a sin. I would be committing adultery with my second wife.

Julia and I dated for approximately two years before I felt ready to even think about marriage. We'd been talking about the possibility as an abstract event sometime in the future, but no firm plans had been made. Almost two years to the day after we met, I saw that a gospel singer and preacher named Ronnie Henson would be coming to Greenview Tabernacle on New Year's Eve. Both Julia and I liked his style of music and thought it sounded like a good way to spend our holiday. The church was not far from our neighborhood, so we decided to attend.

About this time, Julia and I began to tire of all the driving involved in our relationship. I lived north in the Dayton metropolitan area near my work. Julia lived south, closer to her work. The two of us might meet at a restaurant somewhere in between our jobs. After a pleasant dinner, I might need to head back to work at the car dealership. She would drive home to an empty house.

As a car salesman, I worked a ton of hours, and she had a responsible job herself. She worked at a General Motors plant on the other side of Dayton from me and lived near Miami Valley Hospital. The logistics eventually began to wear on us.

At just the right moment, I proposed marriage and she accepted. Rather than wait to organize a big wedding, we like to say that we ran off to Tennessee.

In Sevierville, we stayed in a bed-and-breakfast on Friday night after picking up a marriage license at City Hall. Julia's Uncle George and Aunt Denise arranged for a minister to meet the four of us at 11 a.m. on Saturday. In a very quiet but meaningful ceremony, we made our vows to each other in front of God, a preacher, and two witnesses. It felt great to have Julia become my wife. Everything about her clicked with me. We seemed made for each other.

Back in Dayton after the wedding, both of us felt a need to get back into church. We enjoyed the concert at

Greenview Calvary Tabernacle and thought the pastor might be someone we would enjoy learning from and getting to know. Before we jumped in with both feet, we needed to know if Greenview Calvary Tabernacle would honor our marriage. The last thing we wanted was a church that would dwell on the divorce in my past.

We invited Norm and Tim Livingston over to our house. As ministerial staff, I wanted to hear their thoughts about our marriage, hoping to avoid an awkward scene later down the road. They welcomed us to Greenview and explained their beliefs on the matter. It was not God's plan that people divorced, but that's how things happen sometimes. Greenview believes in second chances, and both the senior pastor and his son, an assistant pastor, pledged to support Julia and me in our marriage.

It felt like coming home to attend church again. There is a loneliness that backslidden Christians feel, particularly strongly on Sunday mornings. We know in our hearts that church is where we belong.

After Julia and I started attending again on a regular basis, I could feel the tug of the Holy Spirit. One Sunday morning, I walked down the aisle in response to an altar call. I prayed through and renewed my vows to the Lord. Restoration and forgiveness flooded over me. How amazing to feel strongly God's love and presence in my heart again.

*"...this thy brother was dead, and is alive again; and was lost, and is found" (Luke 15:32b).*

# 8

Julia's brother David and his wife, Rhonda, came to various family functions. David's sense of humor and positive outlook clicked with me. We talked about our mutual love of cars, trucks, the outdoors, and any number of other things. He made the family events even more fun, perhaps because the two of us were about the same age. In the military, they practically shaved my head. Now my hair grew out in all directions. David recommended I get my hair cut by Sandy O'Cull, who worked at her own shop. I set up an appointment every two weeks to get a trim. I liked what she did with my hair and enjoyed her personality. We chatted away as she cut and styled my hair. Eventually, Sandy moved on to a different shop, Shear Joy.

At one of our family dinners, my niece, Christie, asked, "Why would you get a haircut every two weeks?"

"Have you ever seen me when I looked like I needed a haircut?" I responded.

"No."

"Have you ever seen me when I look like I just got a haircut?"

"No."

"That's why I get it cut every two weeks. It always looks the same, neat and trimmed."

I loved the family dinners. The opportunity to jump in the middle of large family gatherings is one of my favorite things. Julia's crew reminded me of good times with my own family. Perhaps my favorite member of Julia's family at that time was David. He and I always spent several minutes talking about cars, trucks, camping, or one of our many shared interests.

We spent one afternoon talking about the usual topics until we got to a lull in the conversation. As the fellowship began to wind down, and Julia and I prepared to leave, David asked to borrow my truck. This wasn't unusual. Whenever he needed an oil change or other work, I would drive his truck to work. The staff would fix it during the day, and I would take it home with me. He could pick it up whenever he wanted, but usually the next day.

"Hey Sterling, I have a favor to ask."

"Ask away, buddy," I said.

"Would you mind taking my truck into the car dealership?" David asked.

"Of course, I don't mind. What do you need? Oil change?"

"Yep. Also, have them look at the air filter."

"Okay, I'll do it," I said.

"Now, here's part two of the favor," David said. "Can

I borrow your truck? Rhonda and I plan to go down to Kentucky this weekend to the lake. We need a truck with a hitch on the back to haul my boat down there."

"There might be a little charge," I said jokingly. "Of course, I don't mind. Let's switch vehicles now, and I'll take it into the dealership tomorrow."

Although I love my Cadillacs and pick-up, people come before things. Loaning a car or truck to a relative never seemed like much of an imposition. We traded trucks, and I took his pick-up into work, planning to drive it home Friday night. The service department completed the work early in the day, and I didn't think any more about it.

Julia and I spent a quiet evening at home that Friday night. The next morning, we awoke to a knock on the door. To my surprise, David stood in the door threshold looking quite upset.

"David, I thought you guys weren't coming back until tomorrow."

Instead of answering, David burst into tears. Julia came up behind me, but neither one of us knew what to say. He cried inconsolably for a few minutes. Finally, I could see Julia getting nervous that something terrible might have happened.

"What happened?" I asked.

Through tears and sobs, David explained that he'd been in a terrible accident in Cincinnati. Traffic had come to an abrupt stop, and he didn't see the cars ahead slowing down. He slammed on the brakes of my truck, but it skidded into the car in front of him. A car traveling too close behind slammed into David's boat, ruining it. My truck became a boat/car sandwich.

"Oh, is that all," I said. "Are you alright? That's what is important. The insurance will pay for the truck. You are what matters."

David began another round of tears. He came out of the crash a little sore, but with no broken bones. Julia and I praised God no one was seriously harmed. The insurance company totaled out the value of my late model truck. The insurance paid the full value minus a small deductible. David insisted on paying me back the $250 deductible. It's just one more reason I think of him as a great guy.

His wife, Rhonda, is also a sweet lady. She and David made a great couple. I'm not sure if she played the part of the dingy blonde just for laughs or occasionally had lapses in concentration. One time, I parked my semi on Main Street at the church Julia and I attended. Julia's parents lived just down the street. While visiting her parents, Rhonda came in not long after I arrived. I got to talking to her and she mentioned that she passed the church and noticed a semi with its lights on.

"Oh no!" I shouted, "That's probably my truck! I'd better go check on it." Then, she became unsure of herself. Maybe she'd seen a semi. Perhaps it was at the church. Were the lights really on? She changed her mind and decided perhaps she just imagined that the lights were on.

Obviously, I had to go check on the truck anyway. Sure enough, my lights burned brightly as I approached the big rig.

My work life revolved around cars for many years. After selling them for a while, I tried working as a Dealership Repair Shop Foreman/Service Writer. I moved from one dealership over to Stenger's Ford on North Dixie Drive. The job of Service Writer seemed a natural fit since I knew so much about cars and trucks. When people bring their car to the dealership, the service writer asks them what's wrong and writes up a ticket. The mechanics check it out and either find something or not. Then I would act as the go-between with the customer and mechanic, explaining the needed repair and the cost. Some customers would accept the mechanic's analysis, and others objected, sometimes solely on price. I tried not to judge people since I knew what it was like to need something but not have the money to afford it.

As a service writer, it's easy to get at odds with customers. People get nervous when suddenly hit with expensive automobile repairs that weren't in the budget. On occasion, the needed repairs fell in areas that may or may not be covered by the car's warranty. Service writers are trained to understand what's covered and what's not. Things can get dicey should a service writer reject a customer's warranty claim. Often, customers appealed to the manager, hoping for a different interpretation of the rules.

During my time at Stenger's Ford, my manager liked everything to be friendly and happy with the customers. He avoided conflict almost at any cost. If I would tell a customer that the dealership never pays for certain repairs because the fix is not covered under warranty, it can cause problems should a manager come along afterward and cave to the customer's demands. Let's just say this happened to me one too many times. Eventually, I started looking for something else I could do besides working at a car dealership.

"Julia, I can't work there anymore. I'm so tired of being the bad guy all the time. If the managers won't back me up, it's too hard to do my job. Who wants to take the heat from the customers all day long when we are just following orders from the management? Do you think I should quit and drive a truck or something?" I asked.

"Look honey, you have to decide what you want to do for a living. No one else can do that for you. Do what you want to do, and I will support you."

Julia was right. Only I could decide my next career move. Starting something new always takes courage. Those of us who trust in God can access special help with our decisions through prayer. I prayed about the change. Without seeing a bright light or having an angel visit, I still knew that it was the right time to move on.

In 1997, I quit the dealership and started driving for Bradford trucking. It felt exciting to try something new. The company had two primary accounts. We hauled paper and beer. That held another dilemma for me. I didn't particularly like hauling beer. As a non-drinker, I felt funny driving around a big truck full of the stuff. My thoughts ran from one idea to the next, but ultimately, I decided to take the job as a starting out place.

After a couple of years, my truck and I came limping into the yard. Apparently, one of my semi's cylinders kept misfiring, and the truck needed service before it could be driven again. Trucks of that type have six fuel injectors. One did not fire off properly. I told the dispatcher the problem and that the truck needed to be fixed before Monday. She wrote down the issue and assured me that she would pass it along.

On Monday, I arrived for work.

"Good morning, Sterling. You have your regular route today. Just pick up your load at Dock 4 and head on out."

"Did you get my truck fixed?" I asked.

"Is there something wrong with your truck?"

"Something wrong with it? It's missing like crazy. It needs servicing before it can be driven again. I reported it Friday when I dropped it off."

Needless to say, no one reported the truck problem. With my normal runs not possible, the boss sent me out to do a piddly local job that day, and I didn't make any money. Most truck driving jobs are based on miles driven. If in a congested area or only doing short hops between stops, the miles don't add up. Fed up, I quit.

In 1999, dissatisfaction with Bradford led me to a company called TVM. One of the major trucking firms that hauls auto parts for General Motors (GM), Chrysler, and Ford, TVM uses various business models to get all the drivers they need. The company gave me a chance to buy my own truck. It turned out to be a sweet deal. If I could come up with a $1,000 down payment, I could bid loads myself. TVM would get a certain amount from GM (like $2/mile). Drivers like me would bid a lower amount to haul the parts (like 75 cents/mile). GM would only have to deal with one large company, TVM. For their trouble, TVM would make the difference between whatever GM paid them minus whatever they paid the owner/operator truck drivers.

Once I caught onto the business model, there seemed to be no reason to stop at one truck, which I drove myself. Before long, with money I'd made from my own runs, I added another truck and paid a driver.

One of the purposes of TVM's business model is to spread out the risk and cost of its fleet of trucks. By using owner/operators, TVM didn't have to tie up as much capital. It also spread the risk across many small businesses like my own. Work became a lot more interesting as I began to learn the owner/operator game.

*"But thanks be to God, which giveth us the victory through our Lord Jesus Christ" (1 Corinthians 15:57).*

# 9

In 2001, my daughter, Candy, planned to marry. I looked forward to the event with both anticipation and a small amount of trepidation. Julia and I made the hour drive to Columbus for the rehearsal on Friday night with a celebratory party to follow.

At the rehearsal, the preacher walked through the actual ceremony very quickly. No one said anything to me, and frankly, I didn't have any idea how involved I would or would not be in the wedding. My divorce from her mother cast some doubt in my mind about what Candy might have planned for me.

After the short rehearsal, all of us headed out in our own cars to a reception and party. I wasn't nervous, but

I wondered what was going to happen next. I didn't feel awkward about seeing Faye while with Julia. We exchanged pleasantries, and the same feelings of relief flooded in. The two of us weren't right for each other.

I definitely wanted to clarify my role in the wedding, if any, for the next day. Understandably, everyone wanted to talk to Candy, and she spent a little time visiting while working her way in my direction.

"Candy, tell me more about tomorrow. Do you want me to do anything? You know, walk you down the aisle or anything?"

Smiling and laughing a little, she looked me square in the eyes and said, "Of course! You are my daddy. I want you to walk me down the aisle. Who else would do it?"

"I didn't know," I said, a little relieved.

"The preacher doesn't like to go over the ceremony in too much detail. He wants it all to be fresh and new for us. Yes, I definitely want my father to walk me down the aisle."

She also explained that we would have the first dance together at the reception. As a father, marrying off my only daughter felt like an amazing rite of passage.

At the church the next day, I noticed Faye with her sister-in-law and her brother's daughter from Oregon. I hardly knew anyone else outside of the wedding party, some of whom I'd just met the night before.

Dressed in the tuxedo Candy picked out for me, I treasured the moments with my daughter. Before we went in, I smiled and just took it all in. Here stood the beautiful little girl who brightened my life from her first moments on earth. The music changed, and Candy took a deep breath. We began the long walk down the aisle together. What a privilege to share a day that must have been in her dreams since she was a child.

Julia smiled back at me as I glanced her way. My father's heart smiled all the way down the aisle until I took my seat. Throughout the ceremony, the words all ran together somehow.

After the ceremony, we made our way to the reception. After the obligatory delay for pictures, the couple entered looking happy and much relieved that the ceremony part went well. Candy and I danced our first dance together, just as I'd imagined since she was a child. The moments passed quickly, and soon the married couple departed to cheers and applause.

After all the festivities, Faye, my nephew, Barry, and Linda joined Julia and me to take the many gifts over to Candy's apartment. "We are all adults" came to mind again. In a way, this marked the last great accomplishment for Faye and me as a couple. We cooperated to give our daughter a happy wedding day with no drama and lots of love. Candy could now launch out into married life with our blessing.

As Julia and I drove away from Columbus, I realized Faye and Julia would not become friends. Faye, no doubt, had thoughts and feelings about Julia, and I'm sure my new love had her own interpretation of events. At least all of us were able to set aside any feelings of animosity and put Candy first.

Mom lived in the home she shared with Daddy for several years after he passed on. Those of us kids who stayed close to her soon realized that she was struggling with the onset of Alzheimer's disease. I called her every morning just to check in. Typical conversations ranged from fairly normal on good days to downright scary on bad days.

"How are you doing?" I asked. "What did you have for breakfast?"

"Fine, I wasn't very hungry, so I didn't have any breakfast this morning," she replied. "How are you today, Sterling?"

"Everything is going well. Julia is doing fine, and we are thinking about trading cars. I'm headed to work now. What will you do today?'

"Not sure," she said. "I had breakfast a little bit ago, just made cereal with fruit."

"Mom, are you sure you had cereal?" I asked, noticing the disconnect from her earlier statement that she hadn't had breakfast yet.

"Oh, you're right," she said. "I made eggs and toast. The bacon tasted just great."

In a five-minute conversation, she might offer three or four versions of what she had or didn't have for breakfast. This sort of thing troubled me, and I began to wonder how long she could continue living on her own.

One day, she told me that a storm had knocked out her television. Since the aging TV needed to be replaced anyway, I stopped by a store and bought her a new one. I hooked it up and tested it. The TV worked fine, and we went over how to operate the remote control. I headed on home.

A few hours later, she called and told me to come get the new television.

"Mom, what are you saying?" I asked. "Don't you like the TV? You said it was bigger and brighter than the last one."

"Well, it just doesn't work right," she said. "I changed the channel one time and now it just shows static and snow on every channel. You might as well take it back to the store and get your money back."

I drove back over there. When I arrived, the TV buzzed

and the screen revealed only snow. She had evidently tried to change the channel manually instead of using the remote. She had found Channel 3. Regardless of how many buttons she pushed on the remote, no picture appeared. I "fixed" the television by getting the set back on the right channel, then using the remote to navigate to a program she enjoyed. I showed her again how to use the remote, but I had little confidence the lesson would stick in her mind.

Julia proved a great comfort to me and confidant about dealing with aging parents. As I noted when we met, each of us put substantial time and effort into loving our parents. She understood everything that my siblings and I encountered with Mom and Daddy.

On one of my visits, Mom wanted to call someone. After picking up the TV remote control, she kept pushing the buttons thinking it was phone. I finally intervened, scratching my head. My siblings and I discussed what steps might need to be considered.

The last straw came when she tried to re-heat soup on the stove. Having gone to a restaurant with a friend the night before, she put the soup, still in the take-home container, directly onto the burner of her gas stove. After turning on the burner, she became upset when the container was engulfed in flames. Fortunately, she was not harmed, but it scared her and woke all of us up to the seriousness of her situation.

Daddy made my older brother, Woody, the executor of his estate. We all looked to him for the decision about Mom's long-term care. Facing the facts that she could no longer care for herself, he arranged for her to live in a long-term care facility. She couldn't be left at home alone any longer. Each of us children worked and couldn't care for her ourselves.

When Mom got sick and had to enter the nursing home, the government insisted on taking the proceeds of her and Daddy's home as payment for her care. Working hard all those years, Daddy had paid off their house. Somehow, it didn't seem right that all of his hard work went for her care that last year in an Alzheimer's wing of a convalescent center.

Home ownership is a particular part of the American dream. Deciding whether or not it's appropriate to pass on a home from generation to generation may be a difficult issue, but we should all think about it.

The Bible is full of stories of people who died, went crazy, or had imperfections. It's a book about real people with real problems, shortcomings, diseases, and failures. My life is the story of a common man with one big difference. Our Mom prayed for me often.

When I faced a dilemma, Mom prayed. When I got sick, she prayed. When I got off the track spiritually, Mom prayed. She praised and celebrated my successes. She and Daddy comforted and stood with each of us kids through bad times. They celebrated with us in the good times. All of their lessons prepared me for the challenges of life, but also instilled a love of marriage and family.

*"I thank my God, making mention of thee always in my prayers" (Philemon 1:4).*

# 10

Julia's close-knit and lovable family kept us busy. Every weekend, there seemed to be another occasion for a party. They loved getting together, eating, and drinking a bit. Her dad enjoyed membership at the Veterans of Foreign Wars (VFW). An amiable guy, he loved his daughter. Since I took good care of Julia, I became the apple of his eye. Once married and living at our home in Englewood, the parties only increased. Her family always seemed to be celebrating a birthday, an anniversary, or any excuse to eat and laugh together. I liked to bake and cook a few favorite dishes for their pot luck gatherings. Before long, I started to gain weight.

In the Army, one must pass a physical fitness test ever

year. When you hit forty, they start taking the physical training quite seriously to determine if a soldier is losing his edge. Almost every weekend, Julia and I ate too much. On Monday, Tuesday, and Wednesday, Julia and I would diet and eat very little. Our bodies must have wondered what we had in mind.

The family celebrations were legendary. Everybody brought dishes to pass. I baked cakes and pies and cookies. The first big get-together after we met was Thanksgiving at her sister's house. The family's normal routine before my arrival into the clan would be to buy a can of sweet potatoes, dump it into a dish, and call it good. I loved making sweet potato dishes from scratch. I would buy sweet potatoes and slice them thinly. Then in would go the white sugar, honey, and molasses. After baking them for an hour and a half or so at a low temperature, I brought a big pan of them to share. After that first Thanksgiving, they assigned me to bring my sweet potatoes to every carry-in meal. It seemed like a safe niche.

One Sunday, I was supposed to make coleslaw for a lunchtime party. I used a kit that came with dressing included. Trying to lose a few pounds, I adjusted the recipe and made my own dressing with vinegar, mayo, and NutraSweet. This also became a staple.

Through the years, I baked cakes. I particularly liked making fruit cakes. Soaked in grape juice, they weren't your grandmother's fruit cake and people liked them. One of my favorite things to make was blackberry jam cake. The recipe requires sixteen ounces of seeded blackberry jam. This hard-to-find ingredient sometimes made it impossible to make the cake. The seeds give the cake added oomph.

Another favorite was orange slice cake, a recipe I'd

gotten from Carl Settles. He put coconut in it, but I don't like coconut, so I left it out. Otherwise, it is the best cake. It takes three-and-a-half hours to bake in an oven set on 200 degrees. So delicious. If you set a piece of that cake on top of your head, your tongue would slap your brains out trying to get to it.

If there were a lot of desserts that day, we might have three-quarters of a cake leftover as the family became too full of the many other delicious foods. Leftover cake became a deadly vice for me. I might walk by the cake for a day or two and not even be tempted. Then, I would have a small, narrow slice. Then another. And another. Before long, I had eaten the whole thing. So, these years represented happy, family times, while my waistline continued to expand.

While Julia and I lived happily ever after, my daughter moved first to Pennsylvania, then to Cincinnati for work. Her career took off as she served as a representative for a major pharmaceutical company. Her husband worked for an excavating company.

When Julia and I traveled just over an hour to visit them, it became obvious that the two of them were struggling. I didn't know at first if this might be just the trials and tribulations of a young couple. They disagreed about her choice of professions and other seemingly less important things. Candy and her husband both wanted to have children, but none came along. I guess it wasn't in God's plan. I felt bad when they split up. Candy moved to Chicago, again following her promising career.

Julia was working split shifts at GM. She would work five days and have five days off. We needed to sell our house while the market was still good and buy something all on one floor. We put it up for sale with Wayne Davis.

At that point, we had only owned the house for a couple of years. Although we fixed it up a little, it still could have used a bit more work. Wayne activated the multiple listing service, putting us on the market. Absolutely nothing good happened. Not only did we not get an offer, there were few showings. The market felt dead and even the best realtor in the area could do nothing to combat the downturn. We finally asked Wayne to take it off the market.

Julia and I waited six months, continuing to make a few improvements here and there. When we re-listed it at a better time of year, two buyers almost immediately gave us competing offers. After evaluating the offers, we decided the one came from a young couple who had just graduated from pharmacy school. They loved the place and it showed. Due to their circumstances, they had one big contingency. They would only buy the house if we promised to close and get our belongings out of the property within two weeks. Having received no interest when we had previously listed it, we accepted their offer. Fortunately, Julia's parents offered to let us put our furniture in storage and come live with them as long as necessary.

Although it seemed like a longshot, Julia and I quickly went house hunting. We looked at a house on Dawnridge Drive that appealed to us right away. A single-story, sprawling ranch, it had a lot of potential. Our major goal was to get away from climbing a bunch of stairs. As we got older, the allure of multistory living had waned. Still large, the size of the house also appealed to us, as did its immaculate condition.

Could we get another seller to do the same thing we'd agreed to with our own home? We wrote an offer with the same challenging terms. We'll take it if we can have it in two weeks. Like us, they were motivated sellers. They accepted our offer, and we moved into our new home. The whole thing couldn't have worked out better.

*"Blessed is the man to whom the Lord will not impute sin"* (Romans 4:8).

# 11

Life with Julia brought several changes to everyday activities as well as the trappings of our world. She and I worked on my house in Englewood, fixing it up and modifying it for our life together. Neither of us had extravagant taste, but the house needed a new kitchen and some other improvements.

As I described in the previous chapter, Julia valued family. The get-togethers only increased in pace after we got married. Julia had two daughters, Karla and Tammie, who were twenty-six and thirty-two respectively when we married. I loved them like my own daughter and enjoy seeing them with their families. We spent more time with Karla because she lived near us and worked with Julia at the GM plant. Tammie lived in Kentucky.

One Sunday afternoon in 2001, Julia and I got home from church and were relaxing when Karla called. She and her husband Chris wanted us to come along while they looked at houses. Having been a real estate agent, they may have wanted my two cents about the houses they planned to visit. This would have been their first home, and it was being offered no money down, which meant the buyers would only have to pay closing costs.

They planned to attend an open house. When we arrived, it became apparent the open house started later than we anticipated.

"Oh, I see," Karla said, reading a brochure. "The open house doesn't start until two o'clock."

"Bummer! We didn't mean to make you guys wait," Chris said. "We just thought this house looked something like your house. You have it fixed up so nice."

"It's no problem," I replied. "It's Sunday afternoon, and we weren't doing anything important anyway."

"Sterling, I have an idea," Julia said. "You pointed out the house on Sand Pebble Street that we passed a few blocks over, the one that's being offered by your realtor friend. It looks interesting. Let's run over to that house. You can say hello to your friend, and I'll take a look at the place while the kids wait here to see if the realtor shows up to start the open house."

"Do you mind?" I asked Karla and Chris.

"Not a bit," Chris said. "We can hang out and look at the house until you come back.

Julia and I headed over to the charming house we'd passed earlier, having no thoughts of actually trading it for our place. As we pulled up, the experience felt like love at first sight. Both of us just went crazy for that house. It was one of the nicest places we'd seen in our area. Then, as we toured the interior, it exceeded our wildest expectations. The owners had made improvements, and the house showed a lot of pride of ownership.

"Now this makes me want to buy this house," Julia said. Few things made such an impression on Julia. Her excited reaction surprised me.

"Why don't you see if we can make an offer?" I asked. "The price is very reasonable for around here. The finishes are way above average."

"This is kind of crazy!" Julia said. "You've done a lot a work on our house, torn out the wall to enlarge the kitchen, even put in new windows. We have it just the way we wanted it. Now you are willing to pick up and move over here just for me?"

"This is a lovely house, and if it makes you happy, why not?"

"What are we going to do with your house?"

The wheels were turning in my head. "Karla and Chris need a house. They like our house. Why don't we sell them our place?"

Although it felt a little too neat and tidy, we retraced our path back to the first house where Karla and Chris sat waiting for us to return.

"Were you serious about buying our house?" Julia blurted out.

"Are you kidding?" Karla said. "We love your house, but we were looking at this one because it's no money down."

"If you want our place, we will find a way for you to have it," I said.

Long story short, Karla and Chris bought our house on a land contract and assumed our mortgage. We moved over to the Sand Pebble house and lived happily ever after

(at least for a while.)

Julia's daughter and her husband refinanced our old house a few years later, eliminating the land contract and getting their own mortgage. They love the house and still live there today.

The trucking life has its adventures. There is something freeing to the human spirit about getting behind the wheel and just driving. Most of my early trips with my own trucks included picking up freight in Ohio and driving it to Delaware or Texas or Louisiana. Longer runs drive profits, and I enjoyed getting behind the wheel. As an owner-operator, I enjoyed the business aspects of scheduling runs, bidding loads, and keeping an eye on the bottom line.

In 2002, I had a night run to Delaware. The roads weren't deserted, but traffic definitely thinned out as the evening grew later. Back in those days, most truckers relied on the CB radio for entertainment, particularly in spots without much AM/FM radio coverage.

As I drove along the Interstate, I struck up a conversation with another big rig driver. Driving across Pennsylvania, we kept each other entertained with banter about road conditions, the driving life, the events of the day, and anything else of interest. On this particular night, the guy on the other end of the conversation, Gus, began sharing more deeply than normal. I quickly discerned that I'd wandered into a divine appointment. Gus was facing many pressures and problems in his personal life. God wanted to meet his needs.

"I'm at the end of my rope, and I don't know what to do next," Gus said.

"We all feel that way from time to time," I replied.

"This isn't normal stress," Gus said sadly. "I feel overwhelmed."

"There is something that really helps me. Do you want to hear about?" I asked.

"Sure, go ahead."

"When I'm at my lowest, I turn to Jesus Christ," I said. "No matter what I'm going through, He still loves me. It just takes the humility to admit I can't handle everything by myself. Would you be willing to turn your life over to God and ask His help?"

"I'm desperate," Gus said. "I will try anything."

"Just repeat after me. Lord, I'm a sinner. I've known the right things to do, but I've done the opposite. My life is full of problems, and I need help. I'm asking you to come into my heart right now. Take away my sin and show me how to live. Be my Lord. Amen."

Gus repeated those words back over the CB, phrase by phrase. As we traveled through the rolling hills, he became a new person, clean before the Lord.

"Thanks for saying that prayer with me," I said.

"I feel much better," Gus said. "Thank you. I will never forget this night."

"It's my privilege. Check out the book of John in the Bible and look for a good church near where you live. I can't tell you how much God's Word and other Christians have helped me over the years."

"I will," Gus said.

Minutes later, he turned off at an exit, and we lost contact. Fortunately, I know that he never lost contact with God. Our Creator goes with us everywhere. Partnering with God to help someone is an amazing feeling.

Many times during my trucking life, I've talked to

people at fuel stops, restaurants, or rest areas. God knows whether any of those conversations had the impact of my talk with Gus that night. One thing is for sure, my short discussion with Gus had a major impact on me. After that, I realized again how our relationship with Christ matters to those around us.

In 2002, Julia's brother, David, and his wife, Rhonda, went to California. He loved the boating life and planned to rent a boat out on the West Coast. He loved living life to the fullest. This trip represented just another example.

I planned to take a short trucking run on Friday evening over to Indianapolis. A familiar route along I-70, it's just about two hours away to a depot. We did these runs in the evening after traffic cleared. I called Julia about nine p.m. to let her know I wouldn't get back to our house on Sand Pebble until late. She would already be in bed. We liked to say goodnight and just end our day together. The conversation held nothing remarkable. In the 1990s, cell phone coverage was not what it is today. We had a little trouble hearing each other, so I eventually just said goodnight.

About an hour later, Julia called me back.

"Hi honey, I didn't expect to hear from you again so soon," I said.

"Sterling, I have something to tell you. It's serious. Please pull over."

Julia was never one for dramatics. My mind raced as a I looked for a place to safely pull off. At the next opportunity, I pulled off the road and idled down the engine.

"David died of a heart attack," she said. "He's gone."

I didn't say anything right away. Such a nice guy. Could

he be dead at just fifty years old?

"He and Rhonda went out in a boat. Apparently, David got out to swim for a bit. All of a sudden, he said that he didn't feel well. Rhonda said his color looked bad. David managed to get to the rail and climb back in the boat, but before Rhonda could do anything, he just died … probably of a heart attack."

The words echoed in my mind. Neither of us spoke for a moment.

"Okay. I'm coming home. I will be back as soon as possible."

I turned the truck around and returned to the depot. Dropping the load, I headed home. Back at our house, Julia sat with her brother, Ted, and his wife, Diane. Julia jumped to her feet when I pulled up.

"Sterling, thank goodness you're here," Julia said. "We can't get hold of Mom and Dad. They are camping up at Lake St. Mary's. We plan to go up there and tell them the terrible news, then we can help them get back home."

Julia's parents were in their seventies. Julia and Ted didn't want the older folks to hear about the tragedy from someone else. We drove the hour-plus route up to the campground. Their thirty-six-foot camper provided a home away from home. They often enjoyed camping at the lake for a week at a time in good weather. Even in the dark, we easily located them. Needless to say, it turned into a very difficult night for all involved. Julia's parents packed up the camper and followed us back to their home.

Later, we found out that David's doctor had noticed some irregularities. He asked David to go to a cardiologist and get his heart checked out. Unfortunately, David couldn't get an appointment before his vacation. Ironically, his sister, Linda, had a long history of heart issues.

Julia had expected to get such a call about the unexpected passing of her sister, but not about David.

Since the death occurred in California and involved someone from out of state, the authorities held onto David's body for several weeks. Mourning his death without actually seeing him added to the pain we felt.

I felt terrible about the whole situation. I hated it for Julia and I hated it for David. He was such a nice guy. I hated it for his kids. David's granddaughter was born just two weeks after his death.

Although a bummer all the way around, I wasn't shocked or dismayed. I mourned with the family, feeling especially sorry for his parents. Perhaps all things that happened to me in my life by that point desensitized me. I'll never know why it didn't impact me more.

In my religious/spiritual view of the world, I gave more than a passing thought to his eternal soul. Raised Catholic, I don't know what he actually believed. He divorced his first wife, and I knew from experience that divorce can take a toll spiritually. My hope is that he knew Christ and is spending eternity with Jesus. None of us know what will happen in our future. David left his wife a widow and his two children without a father.

After David died, Rhonda drifted away from the family, bringing a double loss to the family.

*"Let not your heart be troubled: ye believe in God, believe also in me" (John 14:1).*

# 12

The trucking business went great guns. I kept adding trucks to the fleet from 1999 to 2008. This should have felt like the beginning of great things, but almost immediately I learned one of the hazards of having employees. A driver came in on Sunday night to pick up one of our trucks. Apparently high on weed or something, he promptly ran the truck off the road and totaled it. I learned to do a better job of screening employees.

Through a messy start, I learned that owning a business is all about overcoming obstacles. Problems pop up, and the owner must solve each issue, one after the other.

We contracted for more and more GM runs and added additional drivers. In 2006, I bought a repair shop to do maintenance on the growing fleet. It made sense to hire a mechanic and buy the parts, which was much cheaper than going to an outside trucking maintenance business for our service and repairs. Besides, having my own repair shop allowed me to prioritize my own fleet ahead of other business. Each day one of our trucks was not in service could mean loss of substantial income for the trucking company.

The first step after deciding to begin the repair business involved hiring a couple of mechanics to do our own work, and one of them needed to run the shop. Since I was still driving and concentrating on the freight portion of the business, I trusted these men to do the required work on our fleet and to manage other truck repair business that walked through the door. Business beyond servicing our own trucks held significant profit potential. When the shop was not busy fixing our own fleet, we could keep them busy working on other people's trucks.

I hired drivers. Payroll ballooned to $35,000 per week. What a kick to see my small business grow until my gross for one year topped $3.4 million. Dad would have been proud to see me as a business owner.

The total sales figure sounds like a lot of money, but expenses also skyrocketed. The company spent $1.4 million just in diesel fuel that year. Most of the trucks were financed, and I faithfully made the payments.

At times, the margins between making money and losing money on a trip evaporated to nothing. The price of diesel fluctuated wildly. On one trip alone, fuel prices rose by $.40 a gallon in one day. When we bid the job, the fuel price might have been $2.40/gallon. By the time our driver made it to Louisiana, the price topped $2.80/gallon. This messed with profit margins and put me in a tenuous position. Pressure grew as our large fleet struggled to find profitable parts runs for the automakers.

In 2007, the rumors about trouble at GM exploded. The company was bleeding red ink, and analysts suspected they might declare bankruptcy. As somewhat of a novice businessman, I'd made mistakes, and I was feeling vulnerable. Since we started expanding, most of the growth was financed with loans. Far from a mature company, the timing for a major financial setback couldn't be worse. Our highly leveraged position meant that any significant interruption in cash flow could prove disastrous.

I leaned on my faith and trusted God, but also took responsibility for our situation. Someone with more experience in the business may have diversified their customer base. As our sole customer, a GM bankruptcy could prove devastating to our financial health, particularly if it took a while to sort out.

My business fell apart the day GM filed for bankruptcy. Although rumored for years, the behemoth automaker and employer of so many Americans suddenly became insolvent. The filing allowed the auto giant to pay pennies on the dollar for any money owed to the many suppliers and service providers up and down their supply chain. Companies like my own were not paid or barely paid anything for thousands and thousands of dollars owed. In many cases, we had already paid the drivers, but would never see our money as a trucking company.

Finally, the official word came. GM declared bankruptcy and canceled existing freight contracts while they restructured. Like dominos, the news toppled many of GM's smaller suppliers and service providers. Soon my company's existing cash evaporated, and the banks began repossessing our trucks.

Adding to the injustice of the way things worked out, the head of GM at the time got a $30 million buyout for doing such a great job restructuring the company. All the little people got hurt, and I served as a prime example.

Flying high and living large one day, it wasn't long before my company succumbed to bill collectors. Those who held my debt forced us into bankruptcy, and the trucks were sold off, one after the other.

As a Christian, I didn't spend a moment blaming God. One day, business was going well. Then, boom, things weren't so good. We live in a fallen world. GM filed for bankruptcy but kept on operating. I didn't feel guilty filing for bankruptcy. Our lenders left us no real choice.

Hindsight is 20/20. If I had kept more money in the bank and lived in a smaller house, I might have survived somehow without bankruptcy.

As soon as the news hit, I started looking for every available dime to save at least part of the company. As I dug into the balance sheet ever deeper, it became obvious that some of my drivers had been stealing fuel. I had trusted people to act honorably, and I was hurt to know that I had more than one thief in the company.

On top of that blow, the numbers for the repair shop just weren't adding up. Instead of growing, the business seemed to be going downhill, even before the GM announcement. First, I learned that one of the mechanics at the shop had been directing our customers to his personal business on the side. If another trucking company came in for a specific repair, he would quote them a high price at our shop. Then he'd say that he could do it cheaper and would charge them a lower price to do the work out of his garage.

When I placed my brother-in-law at the shop to get a better handle on operations, I also found out that the same mechanic invited friends by to pump gallon jugs of oil from the repair shop's 100-gallon barrels. Can you imagine someone being so brazen as to invite his friends over to my business to get a free gallon or two of oil?

Like a gut punch in bad times, this guy, whom I trusted to manage the repair shop, was stealing from my business. Like all thieves, he rationalized his theft and tried to make me out as the bad guy because I should have paid him more, or whatever.

The guys who stole from the company told themselves that I had plenty of money, so a little theft wouldn't hurt me. Like most small business owners, it's easy to trust those you are employing. We assume people will be grateful to have a job and a legitimate opportunity to make money. These guys thought they deserved to steal for one reason or another. The cumulative effect helped take down my business.

As the GM bankruptcy progressed, all of our contracts were cancelled. The sizable amount we were owed would be paid to us pennies on the dollar. We lost all but two of our trucks. I kept the shop temporarily because the bank holding that note refinanced the loan to lower our payments. With the thieves fired, the shop became profitable. I only had one mechanic and diesel wasn't his specialty. I ended up doing a lot of the diesel engine work myself, burning the candle at both ends. I couldn't go on forever like that. After a while, I sold the shop, and life returned to some semblance of normal. Greatly reduced in size, my smaller trucking business stayed profitable and allowed Julia and me to live comfortably enough.

Small business drives the economy. People with the entrepreneurial spirit employ people, which allows them to buy houses, cars, and all sorts of things. The business itself buys goods and services from other businesses. We pay taxes and provide essential services. Little firms like mine fuel the economic cycle.

When small businesses get run over in this sort of situation, many people suffer. I'd made mistakes. The buck stopped with me. Fortunately, I was able to get one truck back, which I continue to drive four days a week up to the time of writing this book. I added another a few years later. With my military pension, my needs have always been met. I still trust in God, despite the twists and turns of my business journey.

After the storm passed, I went to one bank in Dayton that had previously loaned us money. I asked for enough money to buy a couple of trucks. They wouldn't loan me money, saying, "You declared bankruptcy, and you expect us to loan you more money?"

Through persistence, I built the company back up to seven trucks. It's how most entrepreneurs are wired. Quitting isn't in our DNA. My daddy would have been very displeased that I filed for bankruptcy, but it was his fighting spirit that taught me to never give up. What I have today, I worked day and night to make it happen. Dealing with one problem at time, success is possible if we don't give up.

Unfortunately, my business trouble became compounded by tragedy besetting my wife, Julia. After Mom passed away, it wasn't long until Julia faced difficult realities with her parents. Her mother, Audrey Newman, fell sick in July 2008. Just a couple of weeks later, she died. We're not sure of the cause; Audrey just seemed tired and ready to go.

Her passing reminded me of an old saying from Kentucky: "If it isn't our time to go, there aren't enough devils in hell to kill us. If it is our time, there are not enough angels in heaven to keep us here."

After Audrey died, Julia's father moved in with us. Just seven months later in February 2009, he went into the hospital for a hip operation. The doctor said that the operation was successful, and he saw no issues. However, her father never woke up from the anesthetic. Just that fast, both of Julia's parents were dead. Julia and I were reminded that life was meant for living. Putting things off to do at a later time is a fool's game.

Julia's daughter, Tammie, lived with her family in Lawrenceburg, Kentucky. They had lived there our entire marriage. The other daughter lived up in Dayton and worked at the same plant where Julia worked. Julia's first husband and the father of both daughters remarried and moved to Texas. Neither Julia, nor the girls, heard from him much after he remarried and started a new family. Julia's oldest granddaughter was thirteen when we married. Tammie visited us in Dayton relatively often, and we traveled to visit them in Lawrenceburg occasionally. When they visited with us, the kids would go swimming. They loved visiting with Julia. I felt honored that they called me Grandpa and treated me like one of the family.

*"And said, Naked came I out of my mother's womb, and naked shall I return thither: the Lord gave, and the Lord hath taken away; blessed be the name of the Lord" (Job 1:21).*

# 13

Julia began experiencing serious health problems, including diabetes. In an attempt to gain control of her health issues, she considered having stomach surgery to shrink its size. In a relatively new procedure, she listened to a doctor describe a gastric sleeve operation to allow her to lose weight. I came with her to hear about it. This doctor discussed how important it would be to drink water. While it remained her decision, I wondered about Julia's ability to drink the required water. She hardly drank any water at all. Could she make the required lifestyle change?

I took her to the hospital for check-in the Friday before her scheduled surgery on Monday. She was supposed to stay in the hospital over the weekend for pre-op testing.

The plan was to put a scope down her stomach so the doctor could plan the operation. This was standard procedure.

After the stomach scope exam, the technician told Julia to put her street clothes back on and go home. The doctor would contact her later. We didn't know what to think, but we returned home and waited for his call.

As it turned out, the scope revealed a troubling growth. Over the coming days, we learned she had cancer and needed treatment. There would be no gastric sleeve operation in the near future.

For two years, she took round after round of chemo. Her weight dropped from 245 pounds to 175 pounds. As many who have endured this road can attest, it can be a grueling journey. She lost her hair. She was a strong person and a natural fighter. I trusted that she would fight her way through the layers of disease. We both prayed hopefully for the first year-and-a-half. The crazy part about chemo is that it often kills the good cells with the bad. Julia's health spiraled downward.

The doctor told her many things along her journey. Originally, the cancer started in her breast. Then, it traveled to her stomach. Supposedly, those problems cleared up. Then they found new cancer in her lungs. I hoped she might beat the lung cancer as well. Eventually the cancer in her stomach blocked food from going through to the intestines.

A major turning point came when the doctor wanted to put a stent in her stomach to allow food to pass through. One Friday, a surgical team did the stomach operation and installed the stent. By Monday, the cancer had closed the stent, and her digestive system shut down again.

In those two years, we did all we knew to do. It became

a faith journey like no other I'd experienced. My faith is not built on God's willingness to give me what I request, but on His goodness and interest in our ultimate good.

Earlier in her life, before she met me, Julia had a serious blood disease. Her platelet count went down to nothing. She went through a healing prayer line. For six weeks, she returned to her doctor for treatment and follow-up tests. Each time, her platelet count didn't improve. On the seventh visit, the doctor looked at her test and became physically angry. He called the nurse in to bawl her out for providing the wrong person's test results. The nurse affirmed that the test was indeed Julia's. Just three years before we met, her platelet count went from 0 to 100,000 in one week by the grace and healing power of God. She lived twenty-three more years after this miraculous healing.

So, you can see why this later round of cancer didn't seem too hard for God to fix if her recovery was in His plan. I prayed daily for her healing and felt confident. I thought she would be healed. My frequent prayer became: "Lord, you healed her before, and we know you can do it again."

But at the two-year mark of her cancer journey, Julia died. Far from sad, I rejoiced that she was out of pain and now in heaven. I know we will see each other again in paradise. On one level, I am heartbroken. On another, her death does not outshine the beauty of her life or the many happy memories we built together.

I'm the type of person who accepts God's will. Her death reminded me of my infant brother, Gary Lynn's, death just five days after he was born. My mother understandably took the death very hard. She sat in her favorite chair and cried inconsolably for hours. Dad gave her time and allowed her to grieve in her way. Eventually, he went and sat down next to her. When she composed herself, he spoke words that I'll never forget. "Lily, I could sit here and grieve and cry with you for days. If it would bring Gary Lynn back, I would do it. We both know that I could sit here mourning until we both died of a broken heart, but it wouldn't bring him back."

They say that more lessons are caught than taught to children. I caught this one big time. Sometimes, we just have to accept what life sends our way.

Throughout Julia's funeral and time spent with family, I maintained my composure. God comforted me, and I tried to dwell on Julia's joy instead my grief.

Once all the official mourning ended, our dog, Molly, and I would spend quiet evenings at home. In a pitiful way, Molly would sit looking down the hallway toward our bedroom. She had not acted like this before Julia's death. This behavior felt like Molly waited vigilantly for Julia, expecting her to come out of our room at any moment. I shed a few tears over our mutual loss. Molly and I shared the pain.

After a little time, Julia's daughter, Tammie, came to sort through Julia's closet. She decided what to do with the clothes and certain items that represented special family memories. Letting her sort through the clothes proved another step in the mourning and healing process.

After returning to work, I came home at night to fix something to eat. After greeting me and eating her food, Molly would sit at her sentry post and stare down the hall. One of the hardest things for me was seeing Julia's loyal animal keep looking to see if Mom was coming back. This went on and on until the following February.

Just as I was getting ready to go to work one day, Molly

began having a seizure. She foamed at the mouth. When she quieted down, I left for work thinking she would be dead by the time I returned in the evening. I worried all day long. Though not dead, the seizure had definitely left our dog incapacitated. I drove her to the veterinarian, fearing what I would hear.

The vet said she had blood pooling on her brain. Due to her age and physical condition, it would be best to put her down. I gathered my courage, and that's what I did. This final blow seemed particularly hard as Molly reminded me of my relationship with Julia. I lost another part of the family.

After Julia's passing, I did what I always do: I put my head down and worked. I drove the truck and continued attending the same church. My friends at Greenview Calvary Tabernacle treated me well and helped me maintain a sense of connection.

Julia's daughter, Karla, encouraged me to try to meet someone new. "Pop, you're not fifty anymore. You need to find some good church-going lady and get married again before it's too late."

This didn't hold much appeal at the time, but the months marched on and loneliness set in. Thinking about it, I had been married most of my adult life, almost fifty years. I'm a guy who likes being married.

At church, I continued my usual habit greeting people before the services began. One Sunday, I shook hands with a lady named Judy and exchanged pleasantries. Knowing I'd lost my wife and having lost her own husband a few years earlier, she said, "If you ever want a coffee buddy, let me know." Her compassion touched me.

They say when God closes a door, he opens a window. Judy seemed to have her window open at least to friendship. I took her up on her offer, and we began having regular coffee dates. Five years older than me, she fit my demographic. I've never looked at women much older or younger than myself as potential dating material. You might say that I have a thing about age, a five-year range. Five years older or younger is fine, but any age outside of that just doesn't appeal to me. I could never imagine dating someone my daughter's age.

Not too long after I began calling on Judy, my sister, Edith, passed away in Kentucky. At the funeral, I spoke with my sister-in-law, Debbie.

"What's new in your life, Sterling?" she asked.

"I've got a new coffee buddy, a lady I met at church."

"Coffee Buddy, so that's what they're calling it these days."

Truthfully, I'm outgoing and never meet a stranger. Although Judy seemed nice, we both took things slowly.

My youngest brother, Joe, let me know that his daughter planned to marry in June 2018. With invitation in hand, I spoke to Judy.

"Madame, my niece is getting married in June. Would you consider doing me the honor of coming with me to the wedding?" I asked.

"That sounds fun," she said. "Sure."

This represented a milestone for us. To that point, we'd been keeping our relationship to ourselves for the most part. At church, we sat in different pews and didn't let on that our friendship might be deepening to something more. I didn't want to dishonor the memory of Julia, and Judy seemed content to enjoy our time together without making demands.

I finally got tired of feeling like we were sneaking

around. We loved each other, and it seemed time to bring others in on the situation. We talked to our pastor, Tim Livingston, who gave us wise advice. "I think most of the congregation will be happy for you," he said. "And those who aren't … it's none of their business."

In a twist, we decided our coming-out party would be at a funeral home visitation for a church friend. Funny how getting older works. Instead of taking your new love to the high school homecoming dance, you escort her to a wake. When we arrived together, arm in arm, it quickly dawned on us that half of our church filled the room at the funeral home. Several people approached us, both together and individually, to express their happiness that we found each other.

With the relationship cat out of the bag, we began sitting together at church. Not long after, we started talking about marriage. My first cousin, Linda, and her husband, Dave, agreed to be our witnesses. Although we planned to wait until the first of the year, Linda and Dave had big vacation plans following New Year's, so Judy and I moved up the date to noon on Christmas Eve, 2018, at our church. Pastor Livingston performed the ceremony.

Wanting to do something special to mark the occasion, we drove just over the border into Kentucky. Atop a circular, high-rise hotel, there is a rotating restaurant. With a phenomenal view of Cincinnati, we dined on steak and seafood while gazing at the lights. It was pricey, but the food and service only added to the amazing views. We don't splurge on this kind of restaurant often, but it sure was fun to have a waiter with a napkin over his arm fill up your water glass every time it's empty. The dinner and the whole day solidified a great start to the next chapter of our lives.

It wasn't the first time I'd been to that restaurant. I'd gone with my brother, Phil, and some other folks several years before. Phil may have had a drink or two before heading off to the restroom. When he tried to return to the table, he couldn't find us. The rotation of the room threw him off.

As I sat there with Judy, I smiled at all the memories that made me a man who might seek one more chance at love. In retrospect, marrying Judy became one of my best decisions. In the religious sense, I don't believe in living together outside of marriage. From a practical sense, I'm not one to come home and stare at the TV every night.

Both Judy and I want to live life to the fullest. No matter how much we loved someone in the past, life is for the living. As my father noted, you can cry or whatever you want to do, but nothing is going to bring back your loved one. At some point, you have to move on. My mom remained single eighteen years after my father died. That was her decision. I choose to keep moving forward and growing by discovering someone new.

*"Thou wilt shew me the path of life: in thy presence is fullness of joy; at thy right hand there are pleasures for evermore"*
*(Psalm 16:11).*

# 14

In July 2017, I went to my family doctor. After putting me through my annual physical, she looked at me with her most serious stare.

"Okay, I've told you the last few visits that you were pre-diabetic. As much as I encouraged you to get a handle on your health, you didn't follow my instructions. Now you have gone over the line. Your glucose reading is 125. This long after you've eaten, that qualifies you as a full-fledged diabetic. I could give you enough pills and allow you to slowly eat yourself to death over the next few years, or you can decide that now is the time to do something about it. Are you ready?"

"Yes, Doc," I replied. "I'm ready."

"Good. because I'm only going to give you enough diabetes medicine for forty days. You need to take the pills with your cholesterol and blood pressure medicines. It's time to get serious about your diet. Leave off all the sweets. No more pop-nothing with fizz in it. Stop eating red meat. Eat chicken. By your age, you know everything that's good for you and the foods that are killing you. Get with it. Come back in forty days. If you do what I tell you and lose some weight, I will take you off the diabetes medicine."

Her warnings sounded dire, and I paid attention. I'd been on cholesterol medicine for all of my adult life. I know red meat isn't good for the heart, but I put my wants ahead of my body's needs for years. Finally, I felt ready to try eating for health instead of pleasure.

At the end of forty days, my return trip to the doctor went better than expected. I'd lost forty-five pounds just that quickly. Though it's not recommended to lose weight fast, I tapped into God's divine power and really went all out. My sugar returned to ninety-eight by that first visit, below normal by two points, but I wasn't going to quibble.

"Sterling, I'm so pleased with your weight loss," the doctor said. "Your sugar is down in the normal range, just barely. Your blood pressure is also down. These changes are definitely agreeing with your body. I feel comfortable taking you off the diabetes pill, if you are willing to keep eating this way. You're taking eighty milligrams of the blood pressure medicine. If you will take your blood pressure every day and write down the readings to bring back to me, I will cut the strength of your medicine down to forty milligrams. Then come back and see me in two weeks."

In ninety days, I was off the medicine, and I still am. I wore a size fifty suit, and now I wear a size forty-six that is loose on me. My weight went down from 286 pounds to 206 pounds. In July 2021, four years will have passed. I have lots of big, old boy pictures, if you don't believe me.

I was overjoyed. The success begat more success. After the two weeks, my doctor again decreased my blood pressure medicine until I came off it completely. By end of year, I was also off cholesterol medicine. And the best news? Four years later, I'm still off these medications and eighty pounds lighter than I started.

How did you do it? What do you eat? How often do you exercise? The question always comes up about my weight loss. My answers include: I keep my goal in the front of mind; I choose healthy stuff and no bad stuff; and I just go through my daily routine as a truck driver.

My weight loss journey began with cutting out soda pop. Now I drink nothing with carbonation. We all need much more water than most of us drink. I upped my water intake and also include coffee and hot tea. Occasionally, when I'm in the mood for something different, we make lemonade with artificial sweetener. Another secret, I like no-sugar-added apple juice, which can be hard to find. One store where I shop carries twenty kinds of apple juice with sugar of some sort (usually the inexpensive high fructose corn syrup), and they carry no unsweetened apple juice. Most juices come the same way. For variety, I try other juices when I can find them without sweetener.

I haven't had red meat or pork since 2017. The only oil I use now is olive oil. Obviously, I don't put granulated sugar on anything. Natural honey is a great sweetener, and I use that occasionally. The proof for me came on the scale. Looking down and seeing 206 instead of 286 feels like success. Three years later, I only fluctuate a few pounds and stay right around 206.

Lifestyle change requires a clear goal, and I'm not just talking about losing a certain number of pounds. My goal was to get healthy and avoid diabetes. By God's grace, my goal has worked out. Even now, it takes commitment to the goal to avoid eating the wrong foods. The biggest problem with most people is they go back to their old ways. We must change our lifestyle to improve our health. I want to stay this way! I have to leave off the fattening stuff to maintain the weight loss. I feel so healthy, and I have much more energy than before losing weight.

I don't want to have a stroke and have to sit in a wheelchair for the last ten years of my life, unable to take care of myself—not if I can prevent it.

It's unusual to grow up on a farm and disavow milk products, but that's the new me. Growing up in Kentucky, Mom fried everything in lard. It was cheap and plentiful, but there are other ways to cook.

One of my favorite side dishes (for wintertime) centers on fresh frozen green beans. Put them in the oven tossed in olive oil and your favorite spices. I like them hot and spicy. Maybe someone in your family likes things milder. There are many choices. Take a stroll through the spice aisle at the supermarket. Times have changed, and there are plenty of choices.

If I make veggie soup for myself, I put two or three spoonsful of red pepper flakes. If my Judy is eating with me, we make it with a lower spice profile. I add the heat to my individual bowl. Webber makes a savory roasted garlic, for example, with no MSG. It's a good flavor for those who prefer their dishes not too spicy. We also like to toss Webber savory roasted garlic in a bag with French fries and a little olive oil, then bake in the oven. It is delicious!

For poultry, my favorite is Nashville Hot Chicken

seasoning blend. Morton's season-all is also great. Maybe you prefer a little salt and pepper—whatever works for you.

Kickin' Chicken Seasoning is also good for chicken breasts. Toss the breasts with Kickin' Chicken, and throw it on the grill. It makes my mouth water just thinking about it.

Get creative. Try different things. See what works for you. Keep your eyes on your goal at all times. And don't forget about the water!

Recently, a relative said to me, "You've been walking around all night with a bottle of water in your hand." I took this as a major compliment and reminder of how far I've come.

If you face a major event where you know you will be tempted, plan ahead. Our church has an anniversary dinner every year. I enjoy helping to cook for the gathering. At the meal, we can seat around three hundred people, serving them fried chicken, ham, and all kinds of side dishes. If you were to show up about an hour beforehand, you would see me taking a break and sitting down to eat a turkey sandwich. I pre-eat to ensure temptation doesn't get the best of me.

After Judy and I married on Christmas Eve 2018, my life changed again for the better. She is shy and bashful, but she found the boldness to speak up when I greeted her that Sunday in church. Her simple comment, offering to be my coffee buddy, led to a strong friendship. Then we fell in love. She believes like I do, goes to the same church, and we got together. It may not be an unlikely love story, but it shows that hitting seventy years old is no reason to stop living or trying for happiness. I feel blessed, but both of us had to take some risk to find love again.

Perhaps because we were both older, merging our lives

came with choices. She decided to move in with me. She had a house and had to figure out what to do with it. Eventually, she decided to sell the house and give the furniture to her daughter. We had too much stuff to keep it all. She brought her more personal things but left larger pieces for her daughter to enjoy and use. Not having to move all of her belongings or pay someone else to do it saved us a lot of work and money.

At my age, I have learned not to jump into a relationship without a good deal of thought. Due to our faith, Judy and I weren't the kind to jump into bed with someone new at the drop of a hat or outside of marriage. Her Christian values were at the top of the things I respected about her. We wanted to get married and live together happily ever after.

As we developed our friendship and learned about each other, we found it interesting how our lives had intersected before we met. Imagine my surprise to learn that she also worked for Century 21 in the same real estate office where I worked in the nineties. She knew Wayne Davis, my mentor and friend. It felt exhilarating and strange that we shared experiences with some of the same people and similar real estate journeys as well.

In another odd twist, Judy actually worked for my brother, Woody, on two separate occasions. She worked for years in the meat department at Myers, and Woody was her manager. This woman actually worked with my older brother twice! Earlier, they both had worked at a local store called Stump's where Woody also supervised her. It seems so odd that my brother knew Judy when she was happily married to her first husband, long before she became my third wife.

Another common interest, she and her husband loved

*"And put a knife to thy throat, if thou be a man given to appetite" (Proverbs 23:2).*

# 15

classic hotrods. Beyond just attending car shows, they owned a 1934 Chevrolet modified with a big motor. I had owned a 1929 Ford Model A, which I modified with a Buick motor and stick shift to make it into a street rod. I also owned a 1940 Ford Sedan with suicide doors (hinged from the front and back, and open in the middle.) Car memories and our love of old cars gave us much to talk about and a common interest. I wonder how many times we may have passed each other meandering through car shows?

For some reason, Judy thinks I'm an interesting person. I feel blessed. As you've noticed, I have a lot of crazy stories. She's the one who suggested I write a book.

As we got to know each other, I took Judy to Kentucky and enjoyed showing her where and how I grew up. A life-long resident of the Dayton area, it was hard for her to grasp the Kentucky lifestyle of that era. She likened it to the houses on Gunsmoke. Raised in a four-room house with an outside toilet, I have memories she doesn't share. These differences in our backgrounds only add interest to our relationship.

My siblings and I didn't have a normal childhood, at least not by the standards of suburban kids. Out in the country, there always seemed to be a lot to do. Not just chores, but enjoying nature, running around the woods. and swimming in a pond.

On one of our most enjoyable times, Judy and I visited Julia's children, grandchildren, and great-grandchildren in Kentucky. Being with Julia for twenty years, I'm the only grandpa/papaw most of them got to know. Julia's first husband moved to Texas after their divorce and started another family. Fortunately, my "adopted" grandchildren treat us like grandpa and grandma, allowing Judy to blend into our already blended family. What a blessing to go to church with my grands and great-grandchildren, singing songs of faith with four generations.

My hope in life is that someone might see something in my life that will shine out. The love and compassion I show my family, hopefully, will encourage them to live for Jesus too. Judy and I go down every two or three months to visit one relative or another. I can remember one particularly fun and boisterous trip to Cracker Barrel when we all got together on neutral turf. As we grow older, I don't want this precious new generation of children to think I'm just an old man they don't know. Staying healthy and energetic allows me to really take part in their lives and get to know the miracle of each one of them.

One relative calls Judy and me "skinny and skinnier." I don't diet to get attention, but better health is a great legacy to leave our families. They ask me questions, and I hope that someone else will also get a little healthier. Each of us is blessed by God to have health and strength to do what we do each day.

Judy eats like a bird. She weighs 110 pounds or so. Since we've been together, she doesn't cook and bake all the sweets she used to make for her grandkids. We try to keep each other healthy. We make chicken soup or chili with ground turkey instead of beef. Making small substitutions is helpful, if you are keeping your eye on the goal.

In the spring of 2020, we bought a 2005 XLR Caddy hardtop convertible. It went super-fast, having a Corvette motor that did 0-80 mph in ten seconds.

Judy and I also like to improve our houses. One recent project we did together involves the back porch. It used to have a little covered patio. We wanted another living area for the house. So, we tore down the old cover and paid a man to help us create a 21-by-21-foot room. We tiled the floor, and I added lights and baseboard heaters. Eventually, I put in a room air conditioner like they use in hotel rooms. Sliding windows, shades, the room is decked out with the whole nine yards. It's a nice place to drink coffee and watch the snow fall on a winter day or open up the windows and enjoy a spring breeze.

I grow fonder of Judy every day. We are both blessed to find each other. We've bonded together and enjoy spending these latter days of our lives together. Raised in town, she also grew up in leaner times. Her family lived by a strict budget. Like me, she appreciates the little things like being able to afford going out to eat occasionally or traveling to see family in another state. We just feel life is better together.

One of our new toys is a Harley Trike. It's fancy, and we laugh a lot when riding around in it. Shortly after buying it, I sent shockwaves through both of our families with a Facebook post saying: "I just spent my grandchildren's inheritance." Although meant in a good-natured way, I wondered if I made half the family mad.

Seriously, we enjoy simple pleasures and simple times. Our favorite event around home is to have five or six couples over, grill some burgers, and just relax. Losing my brother makes me stop and think about life. Where am I? What is important?

For each of us a little older and wiser, it's time to get on with our life's purpose. If God has something for me to do, I'm ready to do it. If I can tell my story, maybe someone will read it and become encouraged. If a country guy like me can serve God and even start a business, maybe you can too. My ultimate goal is not to die and have the paper say that I left $6 million to the dog pound. I want to enjoy life and help someone know the Maker of us all. God is still in control, and that's a wonderful reason to live another day.

*"...I am come that they might have life, and that they might have it more abundantly" (John 10:10).*

**174**

# Photos

Sterling and Phil getting ready to fetch water
from the creek for laundry.

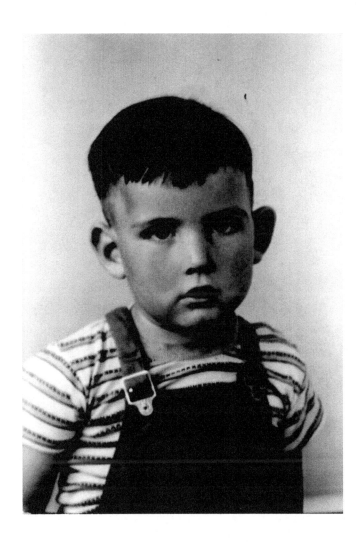

Sterling approaching five years old in Summer 1952

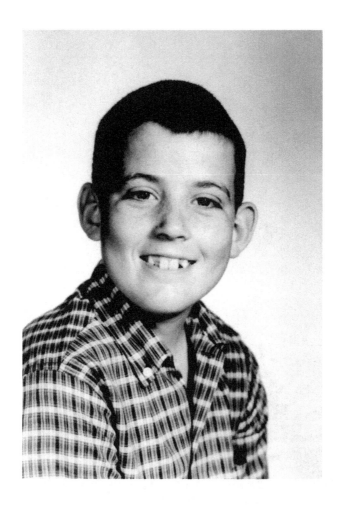

Happy day at Cow Creek Grade School—ten years old.

Graduated basic training in July 1968.

Company driver in Vietnam, March 1969

A short break from work in Vietnam, 1969

I survived Vietnam with Mom's prayers and God's help.

Car salesman for Frank Z Chevrolet in 1972

Sparks Cemetery Road where Gary Lynn Sparks is buried.

Always a car enthusiast, Sterling stands next to his Cadillac
XLR convertible with the big motor, 2020..

Sterling and wife Judy after they bought a Harley Trike.

Sterling in 2021.

Thanks so much for reading Life of a Common Man. I hope you enjoyed it and received something to encourage you or motivate you to make the most of your life. I would love to hear from you.

Contact me via email at **sparksatmybook@aol.com**
I would love to speak to your church or civic group. Contact me at the email address shown above for more information.

Made in the USA
Columbia, SC
18 May 2021